1695

Veils

Cultural Memory
in
the
Present

Mieke Bal and Hent de Vries, Editors

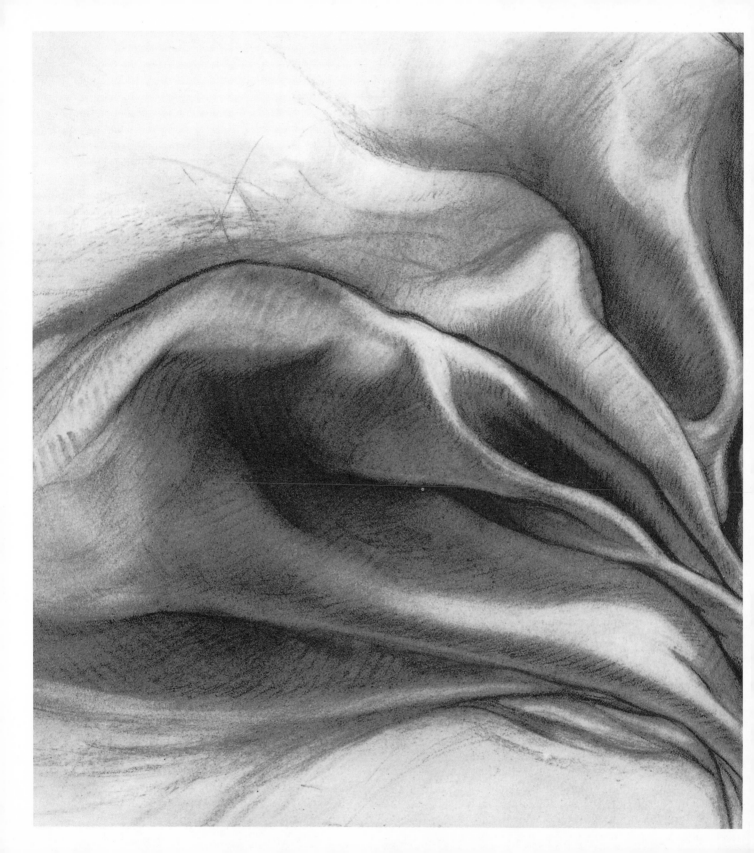

Veils

Hélène Cixous   Jacques Derrida

Translated by Geoffrey Bennington
With drawings by Ernest Pignon-Ernest

Stanford University Press
Stanford, California

Stanford University Press
Stanford, California
© 2001 by the Board of Trustees of the
Leland Stanford Junior University

Assistance for the translation was provided by the French
Ministry of Culture.
Veils was originally published in French in 1998 under the title
Voiles, © 1998, Éditions Galilée.

Printed in the United States of America on acid-free, archival-
quality paper

Original Printing 2001

Last figure below indicates year of this printing:
10   09   08   07   06   05   04   03   02   01

Typeset by BookMatters in 13/13 Garamond

Contents

Savoir

Hélène Cixous

Myopia was her fault, her lead, her imperceptible native veil. Strange: she could see that she could not see, but she could not see clearly. Every day there was refusal, but who could say where the refusal came from: who was refusing, the world, or she? She was part of that obscure surreptitious race who go about in confusion before the great picture of the world, all day long in a position of avowal: I can't see the name of the street, I can't see the face, I can't see the door, I can't see things coming and I'm the one who can't see what I ought to be able to see. She had eyes and she was blind.

Every day she had to pass by the castle. Help came from the statue of Joan of Arc. The great golden woman brandished her flaming lance and showed her the way to the castle. By following the golden sign she would finally get there. Until the day when. One morning in the square there was nothing. The statue was not there. No trace of the castle. Instead of the sacred horse a world of shadow. All

3

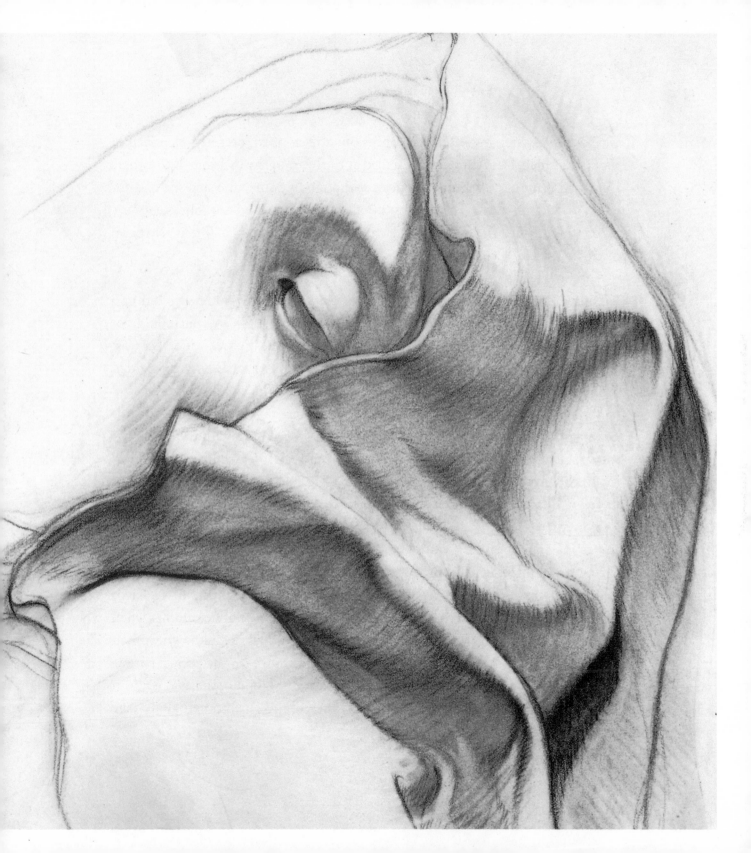

was lost. Every step increased the confusion. She stopped, petrified, deprived of the statue's help. She found herself stalled at the heart of the invisible. Everywhere she saw this limitless pale nothingness, as though by some false step she had entered, living, into death. The here-nothingness stayed, and no one. She, seized up, fallen upright into the fathomless expanse of a veil, and *voilà* all that remained of city and time. The catastrophe had happened in silence.

And now who was she? Alone. A little nail stuck in the gap.

Later in the gap someone abruptly come from the nothing told her that things hadn't fled at all. They were definitely in their place. So was it she who could not see the statue or the castle or the edges of the world or the bus? A little veil of mist had got the better of existences in her poor credulous eyes. The great golden statue had not resisted. This was her first apocalypse. The city lost its solidity.

She had been born with the veil in her eye. A severe myopia stretched its maddening magic between her and the world. She had been born with the veil in her soul. Spectacles are feeble forks only just good enough to catch little bits of reality. As the myopic people know, myopia has its shaky seat in judgment. It opens the reign of an eternal uncertainty that no prosthesis can dissipate.

From then on she did not know. She and Doubt were always inseparable: had things gone away or else was it she who mis-saw them? She never saw safely. Seeing was a tottering believing. Everything was perhaps. Living was in a state of alert. Running headlong to her mother she remained in the possibility of error until the last second. And what if her mother were suddenly not her mother when she got to her face? The pain of not having recognized that the unknown woman could not be my mother, the shame of taking an unknown for the known par excellence, did blood not shout out or feel? Treachery of blood of sense so you can get the wrong mother, be wrong up to and including your mother? Body rage

against those two, those eyes that cannot run faster, their bridle is innate, all the
energy in the world cannot hasten their step. brid(l)e

Truths are unmasked a second before the end. <u>Do I see what I see? What was
not there was perhaps there. To be and not to be were never exclusive.</u>

So as to be able to live, she chose to believe and it often ended in unhappy
discoveries. She placed her confidence in a madwoman whom she mistrusted
but in vain. There is an advantage in the blind confidence of which she was deprived. Myopia shook up everything including the proper peace that blindness
establishes. She was the first to accuse herself. <u>Even with her eyes closed she was
myopic.</u>

Myopia mistress of error and worry.

But it also reigns over others, you who are not myopic and you who are myopic, it was also tricking you, you who never saw it, you who never knew that it
was spreading its ambiguous veils between the woman and you. It was always
there the invisible that separated the woman forever. As if it were the very genius
of separation. This woman was another and you did not know it.

I too was myopic. I can attest to the fact that some people gravely wounded
by myopia can perfectly well hide from public gaze the actions and existence of
their mad fatality.

But one day this woman decided to finish with her myopia and without delay
made an appointment with the surgeon. Because she had learned the incredible
news: science had just vanquished the invincible. It was done in ten minutes. End
of the infinite. A possibility still impossible three years earlier. In the list of in-
vincibles promised to defeat, they had just reached myopia. Everything impossible will be possible, it's enough to wait thousands of years. By chance, she had
known it in her lifetime: her own astral reversal. For all the time up to that day

she had been living in the cave of the species, docile to fatality. She was a prisoner, lunar, from birth; the others had all their wings. It had never come to her mind that she could change her lot. Once blood is spilt in the dust, it doesn't return to the veins. No one would ever have contradicted Aeschylus. Here the blood returned. She was born again.

This is how you come into the world without ever having imagined before that hour that you could ever become an inhabitant of daylight. No one had ever before set their feet on this planet. This event has a date. These days humans change their world every month. There are no longer any myopics through fatality. She who had never expected it had lived her old lives trembling like the warriors dying of myopia before the ramparts of Troy because they didn't even see the enemy appearing three paces away.

The next day as night ended she suddenly saw the pattern on the carpet she had never seen. Then the shelves came slowly up, the first to greet her, smiling. Still yesterday she was the one who would turn her glasses to the left so that the shelves that were never there could make their appearance. And so the world came out of its distant reserve, its cruel absences. The world came up to her, making its faces precise. All day long.

It moved on so fast she could see herself see. She saw sight coming. Before her floated the titles of books, still invisible sirens, and then they came away from the blurred skin and here: they stood out, features drawn. What was not is. Presence comes out of absence, she saw it, the features of the world's face rise to the window, emerging from effacement, she saw the world's rising.

"Am I by chance witnessing the blossoming of creation?" she wondered. Yes. Because it was that day she was seeing, from her myopia that, going away, was still there a little.

Struck by the apparition she burst out laughing. The laughter of childbirth. What was making her jubilant was the "yes, I'm here" of presence, non-refusal, non-retreat. Yes, said the world. Yes, said the timid bell tower behind the buildings. Yes I'm coming, said one window then another.

Is *seeing* the supreme enjoyment? Or else is it: no-longer-not-seeing?

Visible birds passed from right to left in the sky flotillas of clouds ran from left to right, it had never been seen! Come, future, come, you coming ceaselessly, never arriving, come, coming!

It didn't stop coming, apparitioning. Apparitioning carried on.

That's what was transporting her: the step of Apparition. Coming to See. And who is coming? You or I?

It was *seeing-with-the-naked-eye*, the miracle.

That's what was transporting her. For she had already seen all that behind glass with spectacles and without exaltation: borrowed vision, separated sight.

But at this dawn without subterfuge she had seen the world with her own eyes, without intermediary, without the non-contact lenses. The continuity of her flesh and the world's flesh, touch then, was love, and that was the miracle, giving. Ah! She hadn't realized the day before that eyes are miraculous hands, had never enjoyed the delicate tact of the cornea, the eyelashes, the most powerful hands, these hands that touch imponderably near and far-off heres. She had not realized that eyes are lips on the lips of God.

She had just touched the world with her eye, and she thought: "it is *I* who can *see*." *I* would thus be my eyes. I the encounter, the meeting point between my seeing soul and you? Violent gentleness, brusque apparition, lifting eyelids and: the world is given to her in the hand of her eyes. And what was given to her that first day was the gift itself, giving.

9

No, the joy is not to "get one's sight back," but getting to know *seeing-with-the-naked eye*.

What is the equivalent of unheard-of? Unseen? There had never before been any unseen. It was an invention. It had just begun.

And to think that this miracle was striking only her own, her tribe, the myopic.

But if myopia could be expelled, was it then a foreigner? She had always had the presentiment that her myopia was her own foreigner, her essential foreignness, her own accidental necessary weakness. Her fate. And she had left her fate behind with a leap? Left her skin. Her eyelid in which her soul was lying sewn.

Before, she said "my myopia," like: "my life," or "where I was born." One day she would hear herself say "when I was myopic." The beginning was withdrawing into the past. A prehistory has been formed.

Before she was not a woman first she was a myopic meaning one masked. Eyes no one sees behind the glass mask. Oh! she'd fought hard. With against her own foreign body her stubborn cornea. For a while she was the first to unmask herself. The lenses seemed like a fraud to her. People said to her: you have beautiful eyes, and she would reply: I am shortsighted. People did not believe her: they didn't listen. They didn't know. She spoke "the truth." She be-lied her face, her eyes. As if her real. . . As if her false. . . As if she were lying. Wandering, flickering of the lie. Where is the truth. Myopia was her truth.

"I am coming to the world, I am climbing day after day the steps of visibility. Every day diminishes the imprecision of imprecision." Slowly, rapidly, depending on the point of view, she was not-seeing a little less from hour to hour. From what ancient unfathomable depth, running through the nights of billions of kilometers were the visibles coming up toward her? How to measure this slow and powerful advent?

And irreversible.

That's when she shuddered as an unexpected mourning stabbed through her: but I'm *losing* my myopia!

"Quick, miracle!" she was crying. "Hold on! Slowly, miracle!" she cried.

Today the poignant regret that had been the secret of her childhood was dying: she had been the chosen one of the family, the myope among the swans. It was a curse, an internal enchantment, an unmerited impotence that was herself and against which she revolted with all her strong vain strength, the most subtle form of injustice: for this myopia that had chosen her and placed her apart was as undetachable from her as her blood from her vein, it was she, she was it, its inaudible incessant murmur.

Today her sister, anger, was dying.

Suddenly myopia, "the other," the unwelcome, is unveiled: the other was none other than her sweetheart, her modest companion born. Her dear secret. Already the mysterious misty tundra of always was effaced. Farewell my sweetheart my mother.

Now it was time to bid cruel and tender farewell to the veil she had cursed so much.

"Now at last I can love my myopia, that gift in reverse, I can love it because it is going to come to an end." She had fallen into a state of farewell.

The mourning for the eye that becomes another eye: "I'll never be shortsighted again!" But the supplement of lightness in passing into the visible without having to break down the door at every moment. The joy of the eye physically delivered; a delicious sensation of staples removed: for myopia has little claws, it holds the eye under a little tight veil, screwed-down eyelids, insistences, vain efforts to pass through the veil and see: forehead frown.

The joy of the unbridled eye: you can hear better like this. To hear you have to see clearly.

Now she could hear clearly even without glasses.

But while her unbound soul soared, a fall formed: getting away from her "my-myopia," she was discovering the bizarre benefits her internal foreigner used to heap on her "before," that she had never been able to enjoy with joy, but only in anguish: the non-arrival of the visible at dawn, the passage through not-seeing, always there has been a threshold, swim across the strait between the blind continent and the seeing continent, between two worlds, a step taken, come from outside, another step [*un pas encore*], an imperfection, she opened her eyes and saw the not yet [*le pas encore*], there was this door to open to get into the visible world.

Not-to-see is defect penury thirst, but not-to-see-oneself-seen is virginity strength independence. Not seeing she could not see herself seen, that's what had given her her blindwoman's lightness, the great liberty of self-effacement. Never had she been thrown into the war of faces, she lived in the above without images where big indistinct clouds roll.

And also not-seeing-oneself is a thing of peace. She had never had to suffer her own face. She gave herself the loved face for a face, not that she didn't have one, but she did not see it. Except from very close up. From very close up she saw her mouth, her cheek, but not her face. Is seeing-close-up seeing? It was the face of the loved one that was her face.

The blur, the chaos before the genesis, the interval, the stage, the deadening, the belonging to non-seeing, the silent heaviness, the daily frontier-crossing, the wandering in limbo, would soon have disappeared.

Limbo: the region of the myopic, purgatory and promise, dubious environs, the sojourn of the just before redemption. And now she was losing her limbo, which was the water in which she swam. She was being brutally saved. Redemption without delay! But is one saved by a coup de grâce? Or else hit, thrown, struck down!?

—By going, my poor fairy, my myopia, you are withdrawing from me the ambiguous gifts that filled me with anguish and granted me states that those who see do not know, she murmured.

—Do not forget me. Keep forever the world suspended, desirable, refused, that enchanted thing I had given you, murmured myopia.

—If I forget thee, oh Jerusalem, may my right eye, etc.

—Ah! I see coming in place of my diffuse reign a reign without hesitation.

—I shall always hesitate. I shall not leave my people. I belong to the people of those who do not see.

What the seers have never seen: presence-before-the-world. But "before," not knowing that that's what she saw, did she see it?

Do the seers know that they see? Do the non-seers know that they see differently? What do we see? Do eyes see that they see? Some see and do not know that they see. They have eyes and do not see that they do not not-see.

At dawn she still saw herself—one last time—see that she still did not see what later she would see "at once."

And of all that only the myopia-that-passes-from-not-seeing-to-seeing is the witness. But it is a witness that passes. She will forget. But conscious witness? No.

13

Only that myopia of a Tuesday in January—the myopia that was going away, leaving the woman like a slow inner sea—could see both shores. For it is not permitted to mortals to be on both sides.

Such an experience could take place only once, that's what was disturbing her. Myopia would not grow again, the foreigner would never come back to her, her myopia, so strong—a force that she had always called weakness and infirmity. But now its force, its strange force, was revealed to her, *retrospectively* at the very moment it was taken away from her.

Nostalgia for the secret non-seeing was rising.

And yet, we want so much to see, don't we?

To see! We *want: to see*! Perhaps we have never had any other will than to see [*d'autre vouloir que voir*]?

A Silkworm of One's Own

Points of View Stitched on the Other Veil

Jacques Derrida

I

Toward Buenos Aires, November 24–29, 1995

Sero te amaui

So late have I loved thee

→ **Before the verdict, my verdict,** before, befalling me, it drags me down with it in its fall, before it's too late, stop writing. Full stop, period. Before it's too late, go off to the ends of the earth like a mortally wounded animal. Fasting, retreat, departure, as far as possible, lock oneself away with oneself in oneself, try finally to understand oneself, alone and oneself. Stop writing here, but instead from afar defy a weaving, yes, from afar, or rather see to its diminution. Childhood memory: raising their eyes from their woolen threads, but without stopping or even slowing the movement of their agile fingers, the women of my family used to say, sometimes, I think, that they had to *diminish*. Not undo, I guess, but diminish, i.e., though I had no idea what the word meant then but I was all the more intrigued by it, even in love with it, that they needed to *diminish* the stitches or reduce the knit of what they were working on. And for this *diminution*, needles and hands had to work with two loops at once, or at least play with more than one.

—Which has nothing to do, if I understand aright, with the mastery of a Royal Weaver or with Penelope's ruse, with the *metis* of weaving-unweaving. Not even a question of pretending, as she did one day, to be weaving a shroud by saving the lost threads [*les fils perdus*: the lost sons], thus preparing a winding sheet for Laertes, King of Ithaca and father of Odysseus, for the very one that Athena rejuvenated by a miracle. Don't lose the thread, that's the injunction that Penelope was pretending to follow, but also pretense or fiction, ruse ("I should be grateful to you young lords who are courting me, now that King Odysseus is dead, if you could restrain your ardor for my hand till I have done this work, so that the threads I have spun may not be utterly wasted. It is a winding sheet for Lord Laertes. When he succumbs to the dread hand of Death that stretches all men out at last, I must not risk the scandal there would be among my countrywomen here if one who had amassed such wealth were put to rest without a shroud"[1]). Whereas in *diminution*, if I understand aright, the work is not undone. . .

—No, nothing is undone, on the contrary, but I would also like, in my own way, to name the shroud, and the voyage, but a voyage without return, without a circle or journey round the world in any case, or, if you prefer, a return to life that's not a resurrection, neither the first nor the second, with and without the grand masters of discourse about the Resurrection, Saint Paul or Saint Augustine. . .

—My God, so that's all your new work is, is it, neither an Odyssey nor a Testament. . .

—No, just the opposite, it *is*: I'd like to call them to the witness stand, knowing that what they say will always be bigger than the tapestry I'll be trying to sew them into, while pretending to cross through them—for it will be a crossing. And as we're starting to talk in the plane, let's call that crossing a flight and that tapestry a flying carpet. We're just leaving the West to lose our Orient-ation.

—Talking music, you can, *decrescendo, diminuendo,* attenuate little by little the intensity of the sound, but also "diminish" the intervals. Whilst in the language of rhetoric, a little like litotes, like extenuation or reticence, a "diminution" consists in saying less, sure, but with a view to *letting* more be understood.

—But "letting" thus—and who lets what, who lets who, be understood?—one can always speak of diminution *by diminution.* And, by this henceforth uncatchable stitching, still let rhetoric appropriate the truth of the verdict. A trope would still in this case be coming to dictate to it the true-say of its *veridictum,* of this verdict that seems to have been at the beginning, like your first word. By virtue of this strange verdict, without truth, without veracity, without veridicity, one would never again reach the thing itself, one would above all never touch it. Wouldn't even touch the veil behind which a thing is supposed to be standing, not even the veil before which we sigh together, before which we are together sighing. For the same cause, a common cause. Ah, how tired we are, how I would like finally to touch "veil," the word and the thing thus named, the thing itself and the vocable! I would like not only to see them, see in them, toward them or through them, the word and the thing, but maintain a discourse about them that would, finally, touch, in short a "relevant" dis-

23

course that would say them properly, even if it no longer gives anything to be seen.

—We'll have to give up touching as much as seeing, and even saying. Interminable diminution. For you must know right now: to touch "that" which one calls "veil" is to touch everything. You'll leave nothing intact, safe and sound, neither in your culture, nor in your memory, nor in your language, as soon as you take on the word "veil." As soon as you let yourself be caught up in it, in the word, first of all the French word, to say nothing yet about the thing, nothing will remain, nothing will remain anymore.

—We'll soon see how to undo or rather diminish. Diminish the infinite, diminish *ad infinitum*, why not? That's the task or the temptation, the dream, and always has been. You're dreaming of taking on a braid or a weave, a warp or a woof, but without being sure of the textile to come, if there is one, if any remains and without knowing if what remains to come will still deserve the name of text, especially of the text in the figure of a textile. But you insist on writing to it, doing without undoing, from afar, yes, from afar, like before life, like after life, on writing to it from a lower corner of the map, right at the bottom of the world, in sight of *Tierra del Fuego*, in the Magellan strait, in memory of the caravels. In memory of him for whom everything turned out so badly, once he'd gone through the strait. Poor Magellan, you can say that again. Because I can still see those caravels. On writing to him from afar *as if*, caught in the sails and pushed toward the unknown, at the point of this extremity, *as if* someone were waiting for the new Messiah, that is, a "happy event": nicknamed the verdict. Unbeknownst to everything and everyone, without knowing or being sure of anything. The infinite

24

finite time of a trial that consists less in waiting for this or that verdict than in the straits of an implacable suspicion: and what if you were imposing the duration of this trial on yourself so as not to want what you know you want or to want what you believe you no longer want, that is, the due date of such and such a verdict, that one and no other? Not with a view to not wanting what you want but because you no longer want your wanting, whence the interminable imminence of the verdict?

—Yes, but the due date of a verdict that will therefore no longer be the revelation of a truth, a verdict without truth, as we were saying, without veracity or veridicity, yes but a date that is no longer caught up in the fold or unfolding of a veil. Quite differently, still earlier, or later, I see him waiting for an event of quasi-resurrection that, for once, therefore in view of a first and last time, would have nothing to do with an unveiling, nothing to do with what they call a truth, with the dictation of a truth, if you're fixed on that, or with an unburying. What would *as if* mean from the moment—a revolutionary or messianic moment—that I was determining the *as if* on the basis of exemplary phrases such as "it's as if I were alive" or "it's as if I were dead"? What would "as if" mean then, I ask. To whom would I ever dare address such phrases? Now, in order to start a diminution *ad infinitum*, you'd have to write him from the very distant place of this *as if*. For that, with that in view, you have to wait for the Messiah as for the imminence of a verdict that unveils nothing consistent, that tears no veil.

—You poor thing, you poor thing: finishing with the veil will always have been the very movement of the veil: un-veiling, unveiling oneself, reaffirming the veil in unveiling. It finishes with itself in unveiling, does the veil, and always with a

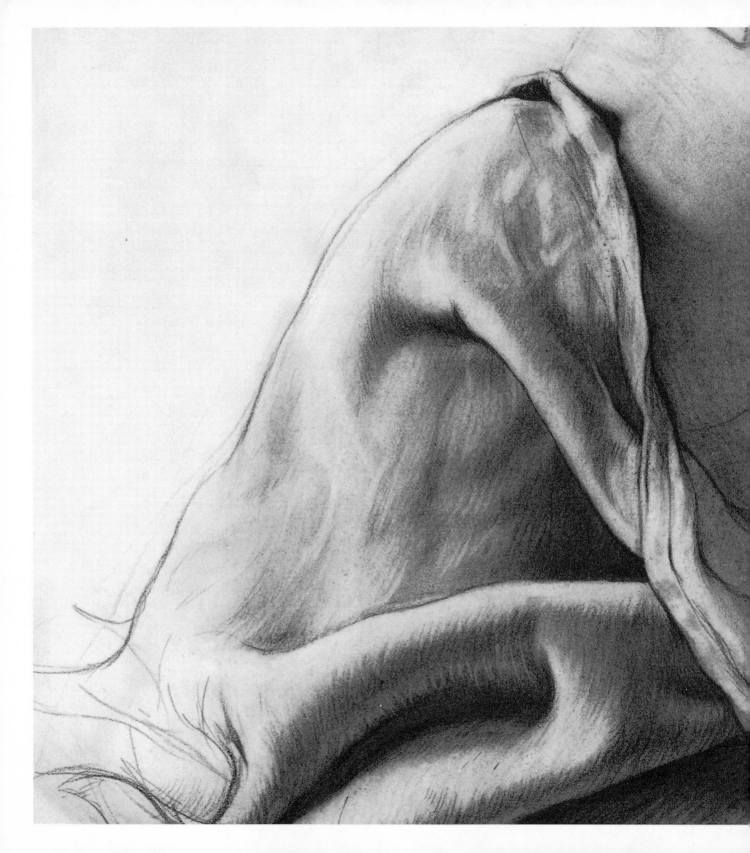

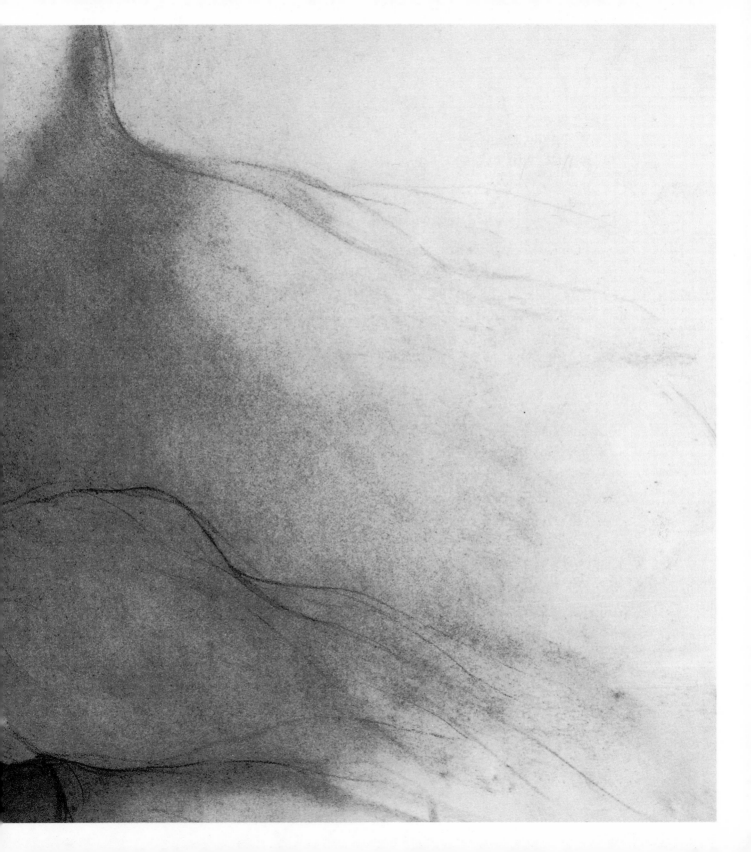

view to finishing off in self-unveiling. Finishing with the veil is finishing with self. Is that what you're hoping for from the verdict?

—Perhaps, no doubt. I fear so, I hope so.

—There's no chance of that ever happening, of belonging to oneself enough (in some *s'avoir*,[2] if you want to play) and of succeeding in turning such a gesture toward oneself. You'll end up in imminence—and the un-veiling will still remain a movement of the veil. Does not this movement always consist, in its very consistency, in its texture, in finishing itself off, lifting itself, disappearing, drawing itself aside to let something be seen or to let it be, to *let*?

—Yes and no. A signature, if it happens, will have pushed that destiny off course. Of course, we have always to remember the other veil, but by forgetting it, where you're expecting something else again, preparing yourself for a form of event without precedent, without eve, and to keep vigil for the coming of the "without eve," vigil over it, see to it that it surprises you. Of course you will not forget that the Temple veil was torn on the death of the Messiah, the other one, the ancestor from Bethlehem, the one of the first or second resurrection, the true-false Messiah who heals the blind and presents himself saying "I am the truth and the life," the very one in whose name the christophelical caravels discovered America and everything that followed, the good and the worst. At the moment of his death, the Temple veil is supposed to have torn. . .

—Shall we say that in tearing thus the veil revealed at last what it ought to hide, shelter, protect? Must we understand that it tore, simply, as if the tearing finally

28

signed the end of the veil or of veiling, a sort of truth laid bare? Or rather that it was torn in two, as Matthew and Mark say, down the middle says Luke, which maybe gives two equal veils at the moment that, as the sun goes black, everything becomes invisible?[3] Now this veil, remember, was one of the two veils of Exodus,[4] no doubt the first, made of blue and purple and scarlet, a veil made of "fine-twined" or "twisted" linen. Inside it was prescribed to install the ark of the testimony. This veil will be for you, says Yahweh to Moses, the *separation* between the holy and the most holy, between the tabernacle and the tabernacle of tabernacles.[5] The veil tearing down the middle, is that the end of such a separation, of that isolation, that unbelievable solitude of belief?

—I know of no other separation in the world, or that would be commensurable with that one, analogous, comparable to that one which allows us to think nonetheless every other separation, and first of all the separation that separates from the wholly other. Thanks to a veil given by God, and giving here is ordering [*donner c'est ici ordonner*]. Whether or not this unbelievable separation (belief itself, faith) came to an end with the death of Christ, will it ever be comprehended, will it ever be comprehensible in the veiled folds of a Greek *aletheia*? No being, no present, no presentation can here be indicated in the indicative. It was, is, shall be, shall have been, should have been for all time the sentence, the saying of God, his verdict: by God *order (is) given to give* the veil, the veil (is) the gift (that it is) ordered to give. Nothing else that is. God would thus be the name of what gives the order to give the veil, the veil between the holy and the holy of holies. Now "God," the name of God, distinguishes between the artist or inventor of the veil, on the one hand, and the embroiderer on the other. Both are men, if I have understood aright, human beings, and men rather than women. But they

29

do not work in the same fashion. Their fashion is different. Like their manner, their hands, their handwork, and the place of their work: inside, within the secret for the artist or the inventor, and almost outside, at the entrance or the opening of the tent for the embroiderer, who remains on the threshold. And that in view of which they work in this way: veil, curtain, drape, is nothing less than the dwelling of God, his dwelling, his *ethos*, his being-there, his sojourn, his halt to come: "For me they shall make a sanctuary. I shall dwell in their bosom."[6] He Who lives there, in this *ethos*, and this Who is also a What, like a Third Party, is the Law, the text of the law.

—Here, in this very place where we are...

—... where we're taking ourselves...

—... where we are going, do I understand aright, it would be something else, even if the concern remained still to distinguish between the holy and the holy of holies. Will you ever give up on this concern? This concern that Hegel, in the tradition of a Pompey he understood so well, will never really have accepted, concerned as he was to distinguish between the secret of the Jews and the mystery of the Gods of Eleusis.[7] Thinking this concern meant also traversing it, transfixing it with truth, going toward something else and ending up forgetting it. An absolute knowledge [*savoir*] will never accept this unique separation, that in the veiled place of the Wholly Other, nothing should present itself, that there be Nothing there that is, nothing that is present, nothing that is in the present.

—Truth, if we need it and if you still care, still seems to wait. In sericulture before the verdict, another figure...

—Sericulture, you mean the culture of silk?

—Patience, yes, the culture of the silkworm, and the quite incomparable patience it demands from a *magnanier*, the sericultivator. Where we're going, before the verdict falls, then, at the end of this time that is like no other, nor even like the end of time, another figure perhaps upsets the whole of history from top to bottom, and upsets even the meaning of the word "history": neither a history of a veil, a veil to be lifted or torn, nor the Thing, nor the Phallus nor Death, of course, that would suddenly show itself at the last coup de théâtre, at the instant of a revelation or an unveiling, nor a theorem wrapped up in shroud or in modesty, neither *aletheia*, nor *homoiosis*, nor *adequatio*, nor *Enthüllung*, nor *Unverborgenheit*, nor *Erschlossenheit*, nor *Entdecktheit*, nor *Übereinstimmung*, nor modesty, halt or reticence of *Verhaltentheit*, but another unfigurable figure, beyond any holy shroud, the secret of a face that is no longer even a face if face tells of vision and a story of the eye. Wait without horizon, then, and someone else one knows too well, me for example, why not, but come back from so far, from so low, quick or dead, wait for the other who comes, who comes to strike dumb the order of knowledge: neither known nor unknown, too well known but a stranger from head to foot, yet to be born. It will be the end of history in this sense. Verdict: end of the end of history, everything is going to start again, and with no shroud we would know what to do with. More or less than—diminished. Enough heritage, dream your caravel, unless a heritage is still looming and expected at this instant, at this point of verdict.

31

—You don't believe in it yourself. I'm warning you, you won't escape, even if the verdict is favorable, that is, negative. At least as for what you will be too quick to nickname "aporia," meaning that, well, in any case the veil lifts. *It's either or.* Either the veil remains a veil, therefore destined to lift, thus following its own movement (and tearing basically changes nothing here), or else you want to undo yourself from it without undoing it, as you've been claiming for a moment, in which case it still lifts or removes itself, you allow it to sublate itself [*se relever*], intact or torn, which comes to the same thing. Two liftings, then, the one no longer belonging to the other but because it belongs to the other, by belonging to the other. *L'une se garde de l'autre.*[8] The one toward the other. With a view to the other. Will you be able to interrupt it? You want to have finished with the veil, and no doubt you will finish, but without having finished with it. To have finished with oneself, that's the veil. That's it, just that, itself in oneself. Just where you have finished with it, it will survive you, always. That's why, far from being one veil among others, example or sample, a shroud sums up the essence of the veil. So you haven't stopped trembling since your departure for the other side of the world. You're not trembling because of leaving, but at what is waiting for you on your return...

—No, because the point is that it is no longer me in question, but what we're here calling the verdict. A still unknown verdict for an indeterminable fault, all the perjuries in the world, blasphemies, profanations, sacrileges, there have been so many. In any case, as for me, I'm lost. But I'd still like it to happen to me and cause my downfall *thus* and not otherwise. Because I feel that the time of this verdict, if it could finally open up a new era, is so paradoxical, twisted, tortuous, against the rhythm, that it could mime the quasi-resurrection of the new year only by sealing forever the "so late, too late," in what will not even be a late conversion. A "so late, too late, *sero*" (life will have been so short), a delay I am complaining about, feeling sorry for myself while complaining about it [*me plaignant moi-même en me plaignant de lui*], accusing, *Klagen, Anklagen*. But to whom do I make this complaint? Would it suffice to be able to reply to this question for the complaint immediately to have no further raison d'être? Is it to God? Was it even to Christ that my poor old incorrigible Augustine finally addressed his "too late," "so late" when he was speaking to beauty, *sero te amavi, pulchritudo tam antiqua et tam nova*... ? "So late have I loved thee, beauty so ancient and so new," or rather, because it is *already* late, "late *will I* have loved thee..." A future perfect is wrapped up in the past, once "late" means (as it always does, it's a tautology) "so late" and "too late." There is no lateness in nature—neither in the thing itself, nor in the same in general. "Late" is already said in the comparative, or even the absolute superlative, "late" always means "later than..." or "too late, absolutely." Before and earlier than objective time, before all metrical knowledge about it, before and rather than *noting* the chronology of whatever it may be, "late" evaluates, desires, regrets, accuses, complains—and sighs for the verdict, so late, very late, late, quite simply (*ateknōs*), always comes the time for loving. You were with me and I was not with you:

Sero te amavi, pulchritudo tam antiqua et tam nova, sero te amavi! et ecce intus eras et ego foris et ibi te quaerebam et in ista formosa, quae fecisti, deformis inruebam. Mecum eras, et tecum non eram.[9]

You were with me and I was not with you.

→ **Will we still recount an eye operation as a story of veils?** I know Hélène Cixous, I have known her, note the improbable tense of that verb,[10] for more than thirty-three years, but since forever without knowing [*savoir*]. I have known her forever without ever knowing what she *confides* here in *Savoir*, i.e.—and this would be, feeble hypothesis, today's revelation,[11] the revolution of an avowal at last disarmed—, that she could not see: all this time she will have been short-sighted, in truth almost blind. Blind to the naked eye up to the day she had an operation—yesterday. The day before, she was still blind to the naked eye, I mean blind when she was not wearing her lenses, her own proper lenses, appropriate lenses or "contact lenses," an expression I like to hear in English, in memory of a certain *Conversation in the Mountains*.[12] What Hélène Cixous has just confided here, she also *confesses* it, no doubt, and therefore *avows* it. But, first virtue in the abyss of such a *Savoir*, the fault she avows was already an avowal, a "position of avowal" in which she (she who almost never says "I" for herself) had lived until then, and lived without seeing, and especially without knowing that one day, thanks to an unforeseeable piece of eye surgery, she would see, she would see without yet knowing what she would see and what seeing would mean. Others would judge that through this avowal, this avowal of avowal at the moment of seeing, she lifts the veil on a myopia that was both a fault and a veil: "Myopia was her fault, her lead,[13] her imperceptible native veil."

—How can a veil hold one on a lead? What does *laisse* mean when we're talking about a veil?

—*Voilà* the whole question, every word counts. It holds, touches, pulls, like a lead, it affects and sometimes tears the skin, it wounds, it penetrates under the epidermic surface, which a veil never does when it suffices to veil one's gaze. *Savoir* could be read as a poem of touch,[14] it sings sight like a touch "without intermediary, without non-contact lenses":

The continuity of her flesh and the world's flesh, touch then, was love, and that was the miracle, giving. Ah! She hadn't realized the day before that eyes are miraculous hands, had never enjoyed the delicate tact of the cornea, the eyelashes, the most powerful hands, these hands that touch imponderably near and far-off heres. She had not realized that eyes are lips on the lips of God.

Reminding us that blindness placed her in a "position of avowal," and that "she was the first to accuse herself," there she goes [*la voilà*] avowing the avowal. She repents of the past avowal as though it were a first fault. In the experience of blindness, avowal was part of the game. It formed part, a first part, a first act, of her blindness. The avowal itself was the fault, *voilà* the sentence, *voilà* the judgment, another verdict, and one miraculously contemporaneous with the one awaiting me, the sentence [*l'arrêt*] of a text that thereby turns out to be the most innocent, but also the most cleverly calculated: infinite knowing that carries itself off in an operation, knowing that knows how to lose itself although it remains infinitely calculated from its title on, *Savoir*, and calculated not to play on its force or to show it, but with a view to outplaying it in what it offers.

—I am indeed playing in my turn with the letters or even the syllables of this title, *Savoir*. In a word as in so many words, and some of them appear to be visible, others audible, in a skein of shards of words of all sorts, a noun, *le savoir*, a verb in the infinitive, *savoir*, a (demonstrative) pronoun, *ça*, a (possessive) adjec-

35

tive, *sa*, punctuation marks, invisible homonyms and apostrophes, *S'avoir*, all that becomes here, only here, in the sentences of this text here, the unique body of an unheard-of word, more or less than a word, the grammar of a syntagm in expansion. A sentence in suspense that flaps its wings at birth, like the silkworm butterfly, above the cocoon, that is, the poem. From that height, the mobile of a bewinged signature thus illuminates the body of the text...

—a bit like the lamp of a hovering helicopter, immobile and throbbing, the flying spotlight looking down, one-eyed lamp watching over the verdict to come...

—... right on the body of the text without which it would be nothing, not even born. The body of the text, the irreplaceable poem entitled *Savoir*...

—Why "irreplaceable"? Must one give in to praise in this way, like a law of the genre?

—No, nothing is more foreign to my concern than praise, just when I am talking from so far away, and evaluation. No, this irreplaceability depends on its poetic act, of course, but specifically where it allows itself also to be ruled, held back, never letting itself let go, by the lead of a referent, an event, the *operation*, which precisely no longer depended on her (she was operated, not operating, in it), a sort of accident, and such a dangerous one, which took place for her alone and once only. The instant of this irreplaceable operation, hers, this time, the poetic one, will in return have cut into language with a laser. That instant will have moved, burned, wetted, then cut up the old-new French language, the well-beloved language whose inheritors we are, but also the thieves, the usurpers, the spies, the secret agents, the colonized-colonizers, the artisans, the obscure weavers, deep in their shop, for it owes everything to us, does frenchlanguage, she to whom we owe even more at the moment we get into it, that is [*à savoir*]...

—Her avowal of avowal gives us food for reading. Food for thought, suddenly, or for dreaming something that's obvious: this pre-operatory vigilance is what will have borne an immense poetic corpus, which I thought I knew and which I persist in thinking has not yet been read: not [*point*] recognized in this century, ill-known especially in this country for reasons that, if brought out, would reveal everything that, in this century and especially in this country, *is forbidden*. Before this avowal of avowal, my blind friend had hidden from me that very thing, that she could not see [*point*], not without glass or lens, the one I hold (and it doesn't date from today) for the most far-seeing among the poets, the one in whom I read fore-seeing thought, prophesy in language, in more than one language within the frenchlanguage. Where we know, that's our secret, what it can mean to lose one's Latin.[15] She had not told me the secret of her every day, and nor had I seen it, or seen it coming. And yet what she declares today has nothing to do with revelation or unveiling. This event belongs to a quite different space, it comes following a different order, that order under which falls too what I am calling the *verdict*. It is neither a torn cloth, nor a lifted curtain nor a split veil...

—But would you dare claim that it is not still hung between the holy and the holy of holies?

—Who knows? Perhaps we have to dare, indeed. As for the verdict thus suspended, what we ought to risk will always depend on a "perhaps." The fulgurating newness of this day depends, or tends. Toward whom or what I know not yet. But it tends and depends on what no doubt I knew without knowing. I was expecting it without knowing: so without expecting, some will say. Yes, a bit like in the strait-time that separates me from this verdict, the expected, feared, hoped-for verdict at the end of the trip to Latin America, on my return from Buenos Aires, Santiago de Chile, and São Paulo. Where one knows nothing of the future of what is coming, before the throw of the dice or rather the shot fired at the temple in Russian roulette. So, what? Who does this re-commencement without precedent look like if still it expects a return? But "resurrection" is not the right word. Neither the first nor the second resurrection Saints Paul and Augustine talk to me about.

→ **Too obvious, that's my age, true enough**: know enough, more than enough, it's obvious, about the truth you're so attached to, the truth as a history of veils. What fatigue. Exhaustion. Proofs tire truth, as Braque said, more or less. That's why I've gone so far to wait for the verdict, to the tropics. From Saint James [Santiago] to Saint Paul [São Paulo]. Maybe with a view not to return. But "fatigue" still doesn't mean anything in this case. Like the "as if" just now. You still don't know the "fatigue" I'm talking about. The exhaustion of this fatigue will gain its meaning, tomorrow, perhaps, from the truth that engenders it and when one has understood what it means, for someone like me, at the moment when he is dreaming of writing it in Spanish, one of his forgotten ancestral languages, from the bottom of the map of the world, what **to be fatigued, yes, fatigued of the truth**, *voilà*, fatigued like truth, exhausted from knowing it, for too long, that history of the veil, and all the folds [*plis*], explications, complications, explicitations of its revelations or unveilings. If you only knew how fatigued I feel at these revelations and unveilings, how many I have to put up with, how badly I put up with them when they are to do not only with opening onto this or that but onto the veil itself, a veil beneath the veil, like the thing itself to be unburied. It's too old for me, you see, too old like me, that truth. For my old age is measured by the age of that veil, however young I remain, and green and naive. I am weary, weary, weary of the truth and of the truth as untruth of a being-there, a *Dasein* that is "each time in the truth and the untruth [*in der Wahrheit und Un-wahrheit*]"[16] "co-originarily in truth and untruth,"[17] in uncovering and re-cover-ing, unveiling and veiling [*Enthüllung/Verhüllung*], dissimulation or withdrawal [*Verborgenheit*] and non-withdrawal [*Unverborgenheit*] of the opening [*Erschlos-senheit*], weary of this opposition that is not an opposition, of revelation as veil-ing, vice versa [*Wahrheit/Unwahrheit, Entdecktheit/Verborgenheit*] as, *a fortiori* of all its supposed derivatives, such as truth as accord, concord, or adequate corre-spondence [*Ubereinstimmung*], *and so on, und so weiter. Et passim.*

You must understand me, you see, and know what it is to be weary, in this case, to be weary of a figure and its truth, of a strophe, a trope, and the folds of the said truth when it plays itself out with so many veils. Infinite weariness, what do you expect, I want to end it all. Protest, attestation, testament, last will, manifesto against the shroud: I no longer want to write on the veil, do you hear, right on the veil or on the subject of the veil, around it or in its folds, under its authority or under its law, in a word neither on it nor under it. With other *Schleiermachers* of all sorts I have used and abused truth—as untruth of course, come come, *et pas-sim*, and of revelation and unveiling as veiling, of course, in so many languages. Go and see if I'm lying.[18]

Fed up with veils and sails.[19] Where do I still get, and from what distance, the force and the desire to come from far behind to have finished with it and pre-cipitate the verdict? Precipitate it without end? And precipitate imminence until the end of time? Sails [*la voilure*] will have clothed my entire history, veils and sails of every sex and gender,[20] more ample than any veiling [*voilage*] of my texts, which have, however, done nothing other than try to enfold them in turn and pocket them, to put the whole history of our culture, like a pocket handkerchief, in a pocket. But with a view to putting yet another handkerchief on top: bigger and smaller than anything, shedding tears beyond being, save—

—Save what? Save whom? You're not even leaving anyone the right to claim that "veil" still has something to hide for you, and that it will suffice for you to have done with the veil to have access to that other Thing itself, that Cause safe and intact. You'd be merely repeating the scene you're trying to look as though you're saying farewell to, making us into your witness, from so high and so far...

—Save that something else already really had to be at work, something else that this old so old history of veils, that tiresome, tireless, tired out history which I'm leaving behind me and which is running after me, a history that I knew, that I will have known too well how to do. Do too well, there's the fault, begin to do too well... [21]

—Exhaustion [*épuisement*], that's all you can say. *Épuisement* does not only re-call the water and the well [*le puits*] of truth, it brings us back to the pit, the chim-ney or the mine shaft, the hole (*puteus*), that is, if we are to believe them, to what a veil is always destined to dissimulate, in the place of the Thing itself. So it's not your *épuisement* that'll save you from the veil...

—But I'm not exhausted at all, me, myself, I'm as young as can be, as though on the eve of a resurrection that has not yet spoken its name. You still don't know me by my name. I am only tired of the veil, it is the veil that is exhausted for me, *in my place*. It has stolen my name from me. I am pretending to confess: failing to have been able to do too well what is beginning to get a bit much with veils of all sorts, as if apparently the fate of humanity, of so-called humanity supposedly born with shame, reticence, *Verhaltenheit*, nudity, evil-knowledge, the knowledge of evil, the tree of knowledge, sin, fall or *Verfallen*, therefore the veil, as though the fate of humanity were again going to depend on whoever holds power over women about the veil. And I am not just talking about an abusive interpretation of the Koran. Saint Paul had something to do with it, we'll have to talk some more about him, and what I admire most in Nietzsche is his lucidity about Paul. Except, then, I no longer know what, not yet who, but that we needed, on return from the ends of the earth and life, something else, which would have an impact [*faire date*], expected at its date and singular like an absolutely unforeseeable verdict, absolutely, that is with no relation to fore-sight, nor therefore to sight. Life or death question, but one that is decided otherwise than by tearing, bursting, lifting, folding, unfolding anything like "veil." This coming would have to come from elsewhere, at its date, like an operation of the other, entrusted to the other, in the other's hand, contrary to prostheses, glasses, lenses, and other lasers...

—But what place are they still taking, these old prostheses? In short, we'd have had our fill, we'd have had *enough* (*satis*, saturation, satire, etc.), if I understand aright, enough of inheriting or, what comes to the same thing, of bequeathing. As for inheriting, a single question today, I see no other: that of knowing whether—and by what right, at the origin and the end of right—knowing whether you will continue, survive, persecute, hunt, hound, knowing whether, and at the end of the day by what right, you will overload the others, become "yours," with your own death, the mourning for your body in ash or buried, with your own winding sheet until the presumed end of time, with the imprint of your face on the linen of a shroud, until the end of time. As someone will already have always done.

—Break with this One without leaving a trace, not even a trace of departure, not even the seal of a break, *voilà* the only possible decision, *voilà* the absolute suicide and the first meaning there can be in letting the other live, in letting the other be, without even counting on the slightest profit from this lifting of veil or shroud. Not even want a departure without shroud and in fire, not far from Tierra del Fuego. Not even leave them my ashes. Blessing of the one who leaves without leaving an address. No longer be onself or have oneself [*s'être ou s'avoir*], *voilà* the truth without truth that is looking for me at the end of the world. Do one's mourning for truth, don't make truth one's mourning, and the mourning of ipseity itself, but (or therefore) without wearing or making anyone else wear mourning, and without truth ever suffering itself, I mean truth in itself, if there ever was any.

→ **Textile, tactile, tallith: tear my tallith away from any story of the eye, from the theft of absolute** *usure.* For after all: before the experience of what remains to be seen, my reference cloth was neither a veil nor a canvas [*une toile*], but a shawl. A prayer shawl I like to touch more than to see, to caress every day, to kiss without even opening my eyes or even when it remains wrapped in a paper bag into which I stick my hand at night, eyes closed. And it is not an article of clothing, the tallith, although one wears it, sometimes right against one's skin. *Voilà* another skin, but one incomparable to any other skin, to any possible article of clothing. It veils or hides nothing, it shows or announces no Thing, it promises the intuition of nothing. Before seeing or knowing [*le voir ou le savoir*], before fore-seeing or fore-knowing, it is worn in memory of the Law. You still have to see it in another way for that, have it to yourself, have oneself [*s'avoir*] that skin, and see it indeed: "It will be *your* fringe, and when you *see* it, you will remember all Yahweh's commandments, you will carry them out. . . ."[22] When one cannot read the original language, one rapidly loses oneself in translations (veils, fringes, or clothing, then panels, wings, corners). "It will be *your* fringe, and when you *see* it . . . ," He says, or, other translation, "When you have this fringe, you will *look* at it . . . ," or again, "It is *for you* in fringe. You *will see it,*/and you will memorize all the orders of I h v H, and you will do them. . . ."[23]

So there would be, on sight, *your* sight ("see," "look"), an appropriation ("to you," "you will have," "for you"), a taking possession. But this is the property (the for-self) that at bottom does not belong and is there only to recall the Commandments. This coming to self of the shawl, every man having his own tallith, that's a necessary condition for the sight of the shawl (you will "see" this fringe, you will "look" at it), but only with a view to recalling oneself to the law (it will be *your* fringe, *yours*, and when you *see* it, you will remember—the law: you will be recalled to the law by the for-self of the shawl). As if everyone discovered his own shawl to his own sight, and right on his own body, but only with a view to hearing and recalling the law, of *recalling* oneself to it or of *recalling* it

43

to oneself. And so to do more or something different, through memory, than "seeing." Each time is signed the absolute secret of a shawl—which can of course, at time for prayer, say the precepts, be lent, but not exchanged, and especially not become the property of someone else.[24] The secret of the shawl envelops one single body. One might think that it is woven *for* this one body proper, or even *by* it, from which it seems to emanate, like an intimate secretion, but this is less through having engendered it thus right up close to oneself than through having already opened it or given it birth into the divine word that will have preceded it. For a secretion, as is well known, is also what separates, discerns, dissociates, dissolves the bond, holds to the secret. One says "*my* shawl" only by obeying Yahweh's order. And by beginning to wonder: who am I, I who have already said "here I am"? What is the self?

My shawl. Mine was white first, completely white, only white, virgin and without those black or blue stripes[25] that are printed, it seems to me, on almost all the talliths in the world. It was in any case the only white tallith in my family. It was given to me by my mother's father, Moses. Like a sign of having been chosen. But why? I say it *was* white because with time it is going a little yellow. I do not know why, but after I left the house in El Biar where I had left it, my father borrowed it from me for a few years. It is true that he still had reason to wear it, and he took it across the Mediterranean at the time of the exodus. After his death, I took it back as though I were inheriting it a second time. I hardly ever wear it (is *wear* the right word? Do you wear this thing? Does it need it? Does it not carry off [*emporte*] before being worn [*portée*]?). So I no longer wear it. I simply place my fingers or lips on it, almost every evening, except when I'm traveling to the ends of the earth, because like an animal it waits for me, well hidden in its hiding place, at home, it never travels. I touch it without knowing what I

44

am doing or asking in so doing, especially not knowing into whose hands I am entrusting myself, to whom I'm rendering thanks. But to know at least two things—which I invoke here for those who are foreign (get this paradox: even more ignorant, more foreign than I) to the culture of the tallith, this culture of shawl and not of veil: *blessing* and *death*.

Blessing: first, for example, the Day of Atonement (and the etymology of the word *kippur* is interwoven, it seems to me, with the whole lexicon of the tallith), a father can thus bless his two sons—not his daughter: daughters, women, and sisters are not in the same place in the synagogue; and moreover they have no tallith; and I'm thinking of this passage of *Deuteronomy* (22:5), in which it is said, just before the prescription of the "fringes upon the four quarters of thy vesture [of the veil with which you veil yourself]," that the woman will not wear the dress of a man, nor the man that of a woman, for whoever does so is an abomination for "Yahweh, your God." I can still see this father, but I could not see him, by definition, by situation, he blessed his two sons one day bigger than he, lifting with both arms his tallith stretched above the two heads. Bigger than he, and one bigger than the other, the sons are stifling a little under the solemn protection, under the roof of that temple so close, during the interminable prayer, in what was called the "great temple," an old mosque right in the middle of an Arab district, anciently judeo-arab, a mosque in the Spanish style since become a mosque again.

Death: then, for example, the same father buried, like all men, in his own tallith. What will become of the one my grandfather had given me if he did not know what he was doing when he chose a white one, and if he chose me for the choice of this white tallith? The decision is not yet taken, and will not be mine: ashes after fire? Earth? Virgin soil with a burial in the white tallith? I ought to have pretended to dictate this decision, but I have suspended it designedly. I have decided that the decision would not be mine, I have decided to dictate nothing as to my death. Giving myself up thus to the truth of the decision: a verdict is always of the other. Life will have been so short and someone is saying to me, close to me, inside me, something like: "It is forbidden to be old" (Rabbi Nahman of Breslau).

If there had been one, what color would have been the tallith of someone who said: I am the truth and the life, I have come, they saw me not, I am the coming, etc., so long after another had said, first: here I am?

2

Santiago and Valparaiso, Chile, November 29–December 4, 1995

Some people are so meticulous as to keep them in a book and make bookmarks of them: since they have served once to accomplish a commandment, may another commandment be accomplished with them!

→ **Fault or election, a veil is worn as a sign of mourning.** Now you've just reread *Savoir*, and *voilà*, for example! What has just happened, change of voice, unforeseeable coming of the other, is this event: eye surgery, an operation of the hand, a hand armed with a laser, so a sort of ray of light, of *Light Amplification by Stimulated Emission of Radiation*. Let's never forget: in the amplifying cave or in the resonating cavity that engenders this radiance, there'll already have been need of two reflecting surfaces, two mirrors parallel to each other and perpendicular to the rays. Two mirrors echo each other in parallel, an echo of light, *in parallel*: one next to the other. Before there be light, before the luminous beam is projected and powerful enough, with a view to cutting, for example, they will have needed, like in nature, this double mirror with two voices…

—Basic question, of the base of the eye too: what is a laser? Will someone one day have to confess that he was circumcised with a laser?

—Such a manual operation can perform what we call a miracle of knowledge, of course—and the author of *Savoir* often talks of a *miracle*,[1] because what is extraordinary here touches on seeing—a marvel of the eye produced by techno-science, but, by allowing seeing in her, Hélène Cixous, at the basis of the joy of her seeing, at the heart of her vision come about but not come back (for it was not there before), there is mourning. At the base of the eye restored, mourning. We have to *learn from her*: a knowing and a piece of news: learn from her that the vision of seeing, her seeing, her vision, was from the start in mourning of the unseen. This operation had to be paid for by a loss. This operation thus engenders the opus, that is, the poem that was born of it and here beats its wings. This celebration poem allows a song of mourning to throb in it—and the party a lament. As if, instead of having long ago to lose her sight, which basically never happened to her, she had just today, at the moment of the laser, and for the first time, suddenly lost the unseen. Like me, but quite differently, she does her mourning for the veil (as for me, I'd like to have done with mourning, she has perhaps already succeeded in that). She says:

> *That's when she shuddered as an unexpected mourning stabbed through her: but I'm* losing *my myopia!*
> *. . . Now it was time to bid cruel and tender farewell to the veil she had cursed so much.*
> *"Now at last I can love my myopia, that gift in reverse, I can love it because it is going to come to an end." She had fallen into a state of farewell.*
> *The mourning for the eye that becomes another eye: "I'll never be shortsighted again!"*

And as always with great blind figures, the sense of having been chosen infuses what she says. It makes the source of each word tremble, it gives strength to reinvent the language in its unprecedented *veridictum*. A bene-malediction elects to genius this great lineage of prophetic poets I recently ran out of breath trying to track, through eye, mourning, and ancestor [*l'oeil, le deuil, et l'aïeul*] in *Memoirs of the Blind*: Homer, Milton, Nietzsche, Joyce, Borges. I would have inscribed her there without hesitation, as the only woman, in this genealogy of night, if I had not been ignorant all this time, these thirty-three years, of the fact that she was all but blind and had hidden it from me. For the operation has less restored her sight than it has deprived her, whence the mourning, of this "malediction," of this "myopia that chose her and set her apart . . ." of the "veil she had cursed so much."

A strait, what a word. Mine and hers. I was talking about my Tierra del Fuego and Strait of Magellan, without knowing if I would come back alive from them. Now here she is having crossed them, and, getting her sight back, she finally hears herself *hearing* and touches *touch*.

Hearing first:

The joy of the unbridled eye: you can hear better like this. To hear you have to see clearly.

Now she could hear clearly even without glasses.

But while her unbound soul soared, a fall formed: getting away from her "my-myopia," she was discovering the bizarre benefits her internal foreigner used to heap on her "before," that she had never been able to enjoy with joy, but only in anguish: the non-arrival of the visible at dawn, the passage through not-seeing, always there has been a threshold, swim across the strait between the blind continent and the seeing continent, between two worlds, a step taken, come from outside, another step [un pas

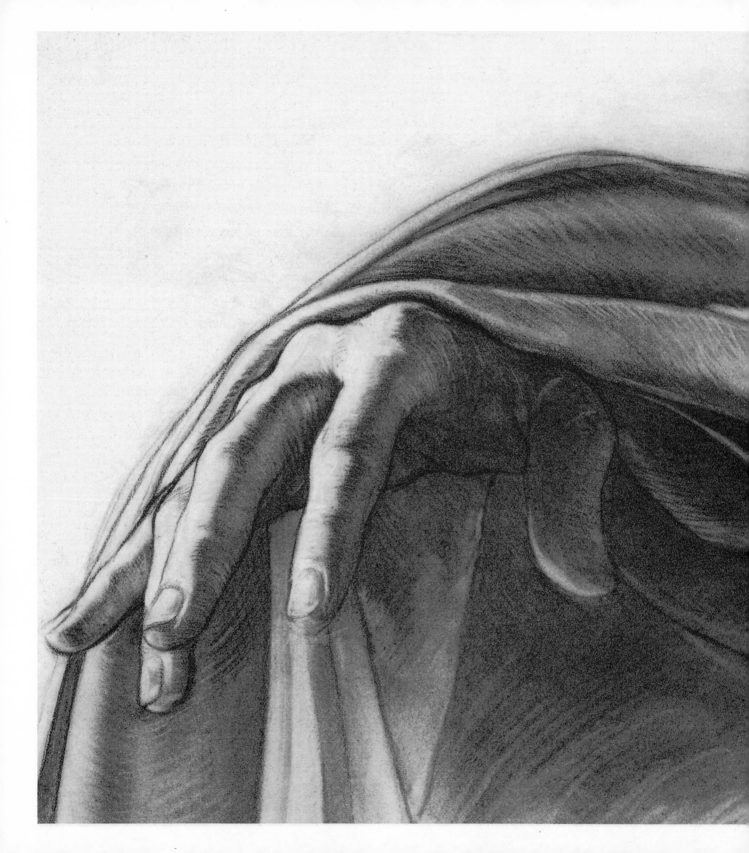

encore], an imperfection, she opened her eyes and saw the not yet [le pas encore], there was this door to open to get into the visible world. ([Derrida's] emphasis)

She also touches touch. First, the "veil from birth" she has just lost, she wears [*porte*] its mourning, and it is a door [*une porte*], the mourning of the veil is even bigger than she is, like the mourning of its truth, its veridicity, under the adornment of glasses or lenses.

The lenses seemed like a fraud to her. People said to her: you have beautiful eyes, and she would reply: I am shortsighted. People did not believe her: they didn't listen. They didn't know. She spoke "the truth." She be-lied her face, her eyes. As if her real… As if her false… As if she were lying. Wandering, flickering of the lie. Where is the truth. Myopia was her truth.

Then the lie—where is the truth. And in depriving her of "her truth," of "the truth," what knowledge, what technoscience with the laser has just given her (the "miracle," as she is quite right to call it often, since it has to do with the admirable and admiring faculty of admiring), was less sight, less hearing too, than touch. Let's re-read: she has just seen with her "own eyes," without her "non-contact lenses," her own glasses which still remained foreign to her:

. . . she had seen the world with her own eyes, without intermediary, without her non-contact lenses. The continuity of her flesh and the world's flesh, touch then, was love, and there was the miracle, giving. . . . She had just touched the world with her eye. . . .

Thanks to mourning, the fire of the New World at last and touch ground.

54

→ **Transfer and translations of the Sandman, that is: an accident can always happen.** The hand of Oedipus, eye surgeon, son and inheritor of another eye surgeon, the author of *Savoir* knows that it can, this hand, be tempted to poke its eye out, her own as much as the other's. He can forget, the son, it happened to him, it's just happened to him, he can be absentminded enough to forget in his eye a contact lens when he shouldn't have, or a grain of sand. The immobile archaism of the fantasy can outplay with its infinite anachronism all the lasers in the world. It can not allow itself to be translated in an age of technoscience before which we must never disarm: the unconscious, for its part, never disarms. It is more powerful than technical all-powerfulness. It resists translation.

Fair wind to translation. To that of the old world in any case. Veils of all sorts belong forevermore to the inheritors of a single tongue, if only they know how to make it multiply in itself. The tongue *is there* or, if you prefer, the velums [*voiles*] of the palate. And with the economy of the so-called French language, what holds truth to veils. Literally, to the letter, to each letter and each word.

In its received truth, translation bets on a received truth, a truth that is stabilized, firm and reliable (*bebaios*), the truth of a meaning that, unscathed and immune, would be transmitted from one so-called language to another in general, with no veil interposed, without anything essential sticking or being erased, and resisting the passage. Now the braid that here links us to the word *truth*, in the language we inherit, she and I, and whose economy we are here and now putting to work *à contretemps*, this unique braid ties the same word, the true of truth or the veridicity of *veridictum*, not only to the semantic motifs of veil (revelation, unveiling, unburying, nudity, shame, reticence, halt, what is untouchable in the safe and sound, of the immune or the intact, and so the holy and the sacred, *heilig*, *holy*, the law, the religiosity of the religious, etc.) but also, *in-dis-*

sociably, to all the formal and phonematic motifs, to all the related vowels and consonants, almost infinite in number: *voiles* in the masculine [veils] or the feminine [sails], *savoir* [knowing] and *vouloir* [willing], *la vérité* [truth] and *le vrai* [the true] of the *verdict, la voix* [the voice], *les voies* [the ways], and *le voir* [seeing], *le pouvoir* [power] and *le devoir* [duty], *la venue* [the coming] or the "*viens*" ["*come*"] of the "*me voici*" ["here I am"] or the "*me voilà*" ["there I am"], and I leave you to carry on without end. It's the same braid, but infinite. All these vocables echo each other in *Savoir*, these words and many others set each other off endlessly along a chain of echoes, in a beam of light whose power is increased by the mirrors it hits on its way, where "she had lived," "in the cave of the species." The braid of phonemes is not always invisible, but primarily it gives itself to be heard, it is knotted out of sight, becoming thus a thing of myopia and blindness. More obvious to the blind, it remains forever, like the warp of this text, you must know it, untranslatable. No one will ever export it entire outside the so-called French language, in any case in its economy (so many meanings, so many in so few words) but also outside its corpus, expanding and which cannot get over it. No one, that's the challenge, will extranslate it from the language we inherit—that we inherit even if or precisely because it is not and never will be ours. We must give up appropriating it other than to put it outside its self which cannot get over it and no longer recognizes its filiation, neither its children nor its idiom.

Don't lose the thread, not one thread, she—another—said, remember Penelope. One thread runs through this braid, one thread she never loses, the thinnest, the V, which, sharp point downwards, runs its genius through *Savoir*. It is not a *velar* phoneme, fine temptation, but a *labial* phoneme. The labial consonant is sung

56

in this poem. Hélène Cixous sings the knowledge of lips. In Hebrew, language is called *lip*. And this curing of the blind is a miracle of the lips. The touch of *Savoir* is a self-touching of the lips:

Ah! She hadn't realized the day before that eyes are miraculous hands, had never en-joyed the delicate tact of the cornea, the eyelashes, the most powerful hands, these hands that touch imponderably near and far-off heres. She had not realized that eyes are lips on the lips of God.

One can scarcely count the V's of *Savoir*,[2] but the lips do what they say in it. They weave by secretion an irreplaceable tunic of consonants, an almost invulnerable tunic lacking nothing, save precisely one word, as though deliberately.

Save which word? And is it really lacking? Who can be sure of it? All these labial consonants, all these lip movements—it is not enough merely to count them, not enough merely to accumulate their statistics, you have to give yourself over to the very necessity of the written at the very place where it falls silent again (read it twice, with your eyes, then aloud, and several times, as here, like this, in different tones). So you must also let yourself be drawn along by the meaning, according to the destinal chance of this unique language. You must *Savoir*. It is done, given, signed. With a movement of the lips, indeed. But also, so that the lips be-come at last visible and tangible, so that they may touch each other, so that they may be no longer loudspeakers or spokespersons [*porte-voix ou porte-parole*], she signs with a movement of lips that separate on touching, in the hiatus or the gape of a strange silence.

Omitted, for one word is omitted, I do indeed say omitted, doubtless omitted deliberately, *la voile* [sail] is not named. Does that mean there is no sail? And that *Savoir* is ignoring it? No, *Savoir* knows how to ignore it with its learned ignorance.

There is a spectacular homonymy, one that works in French, only in French, and even more orthographical than that between *soi* [self] and *soie* [silk]: between *voile* and *voile*, *le* voile and *la* voile. This homonymy that is effaced in pluralizing itself, *les voiles*, or in making itself indefinite, *quelque voile* (some veil, some sail), this homonymy one can play like gender difference, or sex in grammar, that's the only possibility, as you have been able to admire, that *Savoir* does not put to work. Unless that's all it's thinking about. *La voile*, that's the only possibility that a *Savoir* does not exhibit. It does not unfold it *explicitly*, and that's the whole question, the whole art of weaving and braiding that the tradition thinks it ought to reserve for women. It made a certain Freud dream, where he was not far from admitting the fantasy, and even the *idée fixe*, precisely on the subject of a modesty that was feminine, more feminine, feminine rather than not, come along to "hide" (*verdecken*) a certain "lack of penis" (*Penismangel*). If I am in that case prey to a fantasy or an *idée fixe* about this, confesses the man, for it is also a confession, "I am naturally without defense" (*natürlich wehrlos*), disarmed, unarmed.

[Great and inexhaustible penelopean scene that is played in the tissue of this text, for it is also a *text*, on *Femininity*... (Is it unfair to see in it the matrix of all the Lacanian theorems on a libido supposedly only masculine, on a phallus that, unlike the penis, belongs to no sex, and on castration, and truth, and the veil and the cause?) Freud's reference to braiding (*Flechten*) or weaving (*Weben*) closely follows the statement according to which "there is only one libido," but in the service of both sexual functions, so that we can assign it no sex, unless, adds Freud, relying too much on the conventional equivalence of activity and virility, one says that it is masculine. But in that case never forget, he goes on more precisely still, that this libido comprises "tendencies with passive aims." In any case, if one can in a pinch invoke a masculine libido, Freud insists, there is no sense and no justification in talking about a "feminine libido." After which, with a certain prudence, alleging imputations, commonly accepted truths, but also the necessity of distinguishing between the sexual function and discipline or social education, Freud mentions successively the frequency of feminine frigidity, the development of feminine narcissism [Psyche, you'll say, or the woman with the built-in mirror: the laser, see above!], and especially modesty (*pudeur*; *Scham*), which passes for a feminine property par excellence. In these two last cases, the cause does not appear to be in doubt for Freud: "penis envy," penis envy I say, late compensation for an "originary" sexual inferiority, maneuver with a view to hide (*verdecken*) a "defect of the genital organs." Freud's metalanguage then resorts to the opposable figures of hiding or veiling (*verdecken, verhüllen*) on the one hand, and of uncovering (*Entdeckung, Erfindung*) on the other, still with a view to analyzing the motivations that might push the woman to invent, discover, unveil—and hide. No doubt one thinks that women have contributed little to the history of civilization by their "discoveries and inventions" (*Entdeckungen und Erfindungen*). But they have discovered (*erfunden*), uncovered one technique, that of braiding and weaving. The unconscious motive of this "discovery"? Hiding, veiling a "defect of the genital organs." So they *discovered with a view to veiling*. They have unveiled the means of veiling. In truth, looking more closely, over Freud's shoulder, they have discovered *nothing at all*, all they did was imitate, since Nature, dame "Nature," making pubic hair grow at puberty, had already "given," he says, a model, a paradigm (*Vorbild*) for what was basically only an "imitation" (*Nachahmung*). This pubic hair already hides, it dissimulates, it veils (*verhüllt*) the genital organs. For this feminine "technique," only one further "step" was necessary: make the threads

59

or fibers (*Fasern*) hold together, intertwine them from where they were stuck on the body right on the skin, merely bushy, mixed up, felted (*verfilzt*).

But what authorizes Freud to speak here, against the very logic of his argument, of a "technique"? Is it still an art or an artifice, is it a discovery, this so-called "technique" that invents only the means of imitating nature, and in truth of unfolding, making explicit, unveiling a natural movement of nature? And unveiling a movement that itself consists in veiling? Of decrypting a nature that, as is well known, likes to encrypt (itself), *physis kruptesthai philei*? This "technique" is less a break with *physis* than an imitative extension of it, thus confirming, perhaps, a certain animality of woman even in her artifices. (And what if a *tekhnè* never broke radically with a *physis*, if it only ever deferred it in differing from it, why reserve this animal naturality to woman?) A woman would weave like a body secretes for itself its own textile, like a worm, but this time like a worm without worm, a worm primarily concerned to hide in itself its non-being. What the woman would like to veil, according to Freud who, of course, does not mention the animal here, is that she does not have the worm she perhaps is. (I do not know what can be done with this piece of data, but in German one says *Fasernackt* for "naked as a worm" or "starkers.") Freud's conclusion, which I have already quoted, would deserve interminable analysis. It calls on the reader to witness: "If you reject this idea as imaginary [as a fantastical fantasy, *als phantastisch*], and if you impute to me as an *idée fixe* [*als eine fixe Idee*] the influence of the lack of a penis on the formation of femininity, then I am naturally disarmed (*natürlich wehrlos*)." Freud names arms (*Wehr*). He is not, supposedly is not, without the truth of the true (*Wahrlos*, if you like) but without arms (*wehrlos*) and naturally "naturally" (*natürlich*) disarmed, vulnerable, naked.

What should we retain from this rhetoric? What should we conclude from this last hypothesis in the form of a fictive avowal? At least this: the fantasy can be in this case an arm (*Wehr*), and the arm a fantasy. And without getting to the bottom of things here (where the question of the bottom and the bottomless bottom remains entire), let us propose a protocol or a premise for any discussion that may happen: perhaps we should no longer exclude the possibility that, instead of simply being opposites or being mutually exclusive, both the truth (to be unveiled) and the fantasy and the arm be *on the same side*. Instead of having to choose between two sides, one having a bone to pick [*maille à partir*, a "stitch to separate"] with the other, we would have to find out how to get by on the side of this same, on the side of the same rib [*du côté de la même côte*] (man woman) when it can always become coat of mail [*cotte de maille*] or an uneasy settlement [*cote mal taillée*]. We have to disentangle, disencumber, extricate before opposing absence to presence: of the Penis, of the Phallus, of the Thing or the Cause behind the Veil.

In counterpoint to "Femininity," that New "Introductory" Lecture on Psychoanalysis, I will here counsel reading or re-reading *La*.[3] Here Hélène Cixous deals in her poetic and thinking way, getting her hands and languages involved, with all these huge questions. I can only quote a few lines of what is more, in truth, than a counterpoint; but this to incite you to read it all, for quoting is not reading, and it would not suffice to recall the innumerable veils of *La*, "the children with veiled faces,"[4] the equivocal multiplicity or the enveloped duplicity of sexes ("And under the sheet who knows what sexes are rocked, are troubled?"[5]), it would also be necessary to deploy too the innumerable folds of a reply to *this* Freud, the one of the equivalence mother=matter=*materia*=Madeira=*Holz*=*hylè*, etc., who is none other than the Freud of *Penismangel* and the pseudo-discovery of weaving:

. . . Madeira!

She exhibits her primary content, her crowns of veils, of branches, her vegetable furs, and makes possible and inevitable the work of the languages that cover her in words of love. Which elaborate the matters she is made of in all technical, filial, artistic, linguistic manners, as its pressing charm suggests, precisely.

Mysteriously, imposes it.

As though the future were inscribed There. In front of her, almost visible. And yet already inscribed in all the languages.

And then everything that is written under the title "Being her butterfly" ("Toward the bed of straw, of fur, of fresh straw buzzing toward the bisexual bed. . . ."[6]), and then the discovery of sight foreseen in the work twenty years before the "operation," when "sight" means as much the sight of the other as my own, that I see you and that you see, and that you can see me also see you see me, in the double mirror before all lasers:

I am coming! I'm getting there! I am in sight of you, and of seeing you, I see!
So I had never seen anything, the suns were rising for nothing!
Your sight! Your sight! Oh naked! [Ta vue! Ta vue! Oh nue!][7]

And finally for what is without end, this speech in *L'amie de l'abîme*:

Often her abyss becomes for her an arm in the struggle against the pursuer. . . .
In truth, the abyss is as natural for her as her family relation with the infinite. She is herself a mixture of edge, abyss, and leap into the infinite. But natural feminine leap.
How does a girl jump? Without calculating, without measuring the abyss, without preparation. Let's start with the leaps of the Maid. . . .

The rider sees he is lost.

(You have to wonder over whom the young rider is going to jump. Every woman will have guessed that the lion is none other than the figure of the Scolding Master. See his Introductory Lectures on Psychoanalysis.)[8]

The great art of *Savoir*, one might say then, is this: not to name *la voile*, reticence and modesty, stop there, know how not to go too far, how to hold in reserve what would be too visible, and keep it *silent*, another way of veiling, of veiling one's voice. How can one speak of a veiled voice,[9] still veiled even in song, and even when shouting? *Savoir*: prefer diminution, in the *keeping silent* of reticence, that is, that figure of rhetoric that consists in saying more through silence than eloquence itself. The sails of Tristan and Isolde, Hélène Cixous has renamed them elsewhere[10] veils in the feminine. There is indeed the covering of "eyelids," there is indeed a *voilette*, in *Savoir*, a feminine "voilette de brume," but not sails caught in the wind, the sails of sailing, the sails of gliding, the sails of the caravels. It is true that there are wings: ". . . the others had all their wings." And we know with this knowledge that if we have to count on absence, there can be no question of counting here presences and absences. There is no table to table them, no slide rule for this knowledge.

→ **All my nicknames, I have so many: what I am nicknaming here the tallith, my tallith, my own tallith, my very own,** is not a veil, nor a sail—nor a canvas [*toile*], it's a prayer shawl.

It is unique. I think I never talk to it, but it is unique, I know that and it knows that I know and it knows that I know without my having to tell it, that it is unique. It doesn't speak either but it could, we both know that.

Liaison or alliance with the unpronounceable. My tallith does not cover my whole body and leaves me vulnerable. I belong to it and I live in it before claiming it as my property. Perhaps it gives me in secret, I don't know, a roof or protection but, far from assuring me of anything at all, it recalls me to the mortal wound. Recalling me thus, everything in it recalls me to the "One," the "only once," "for one only." Unlike a veil, at least this is what I would like to teach or say in myself, this tallith depends on the One of the unique, the singular event whose repetition repeats only, and that's history, the "once only" of the Law given, the 613 or so commandments that make up the Law (they say that the numerical value of the word designating the fringes of the tallith, the tzitziths, is 600, plus 8 threads and 5 knots, making 613).

Before hiding from sight like an opaque veil,
before letting light through like a translucent veil
before showing the thing like a transparent veil
before hinting to sight like a veil that lets one make out, through the diaphanous light, the thing and the forms it is embracing,
before all else, my tallith touches itself.

We indeed say "before," "before all else," in front of everything, for that does not mean that the tallith and its fringes have simply nothing to do with seeing. Simply one sees them and one sees *through* them differently than (*through*) a veil or behind a veil to be lifted.[11] Before and in front of the veil. This tactile thing is not properly speaking or *stricto sensu* a textile, not yet or already no longer. Nor is it worn like a tunic but, as tactile, tactile before being visible, like a blind person's thing. Right on the body or far from the body. When it is worn right on the body, the tallith *touches itself* like the sacred texts of the tefillin (phylacteries). Sometimes on top of, sometimes underneath, the other clothes. Underneath, that's the one I never had, the little one, they call it, the one you should wear all day. One can sleep in the little tallith, so I've never done that. If one has slept in the little tallith, one does not have to bless it on getting up. But the blessing for the big tallith must in that case include the little one. In a book my father left me, I learn that if one must of course take off one's tallith to go "to the lavatory," one does not have to bless it when one puts it back on, since "going to the lavatory" "is not an interruption." I also learn that a tallith must be cut to the prescribed size and above all woven of white sheep's wool.

White sheep's wool: this last recommendation appears to be a major one. To understand it, one must untangle the threads of more texts or make sense of more prescriptions than I can decipher here. For this point appears to be a point of dispute, if not of controversy. I am not sure that my tallith is made of pure and "natural" silk (what's natural silk?), but I do believe that it is made of neither linen nor wool. In truth, I'm starting to fear not. When one is obliged to make do with a linen tallith on which it is impossible to attach woolen fringes, some people claim that in that case you must sew leather corners on—skin, basically—and then sew woolen fringes onto this animal skin. The impossibility, or what is really the forbidding of woolen fringes directly on the linen tallith, in this case, could come from certain prescriptions in Deuteronomy (2:2) concerning the sheep, the lamb, the tunic of brother and neighbor. I believe I have already said that women do not have a tallith, but I do not know who makes the tallith. In the same passage of Deuteronomy—*Words*, in Chouraqui's translation—the following verse solemnly forbids both men and women, as an "abom-

ination for Yahweh, your God," from exchanging their clothes. Their "tunic"
says Chouraqui: "Man's clothes will not be on a woman, man will not put on a
woman's tunic: yes, whoever does that is in abomination for I h v H, ^{adonaï} your
Elohim."

At the moment of transcribing this transcription, as faithfully as I can, I look
at these sacred letters, these blessed letters [*ces lettres sacrées, ces sacrées lettres*], I
stare at the acronym of these consonants: I H V H. Both immobile and mobile,
without possible permutation, the holy acronym never trembles, it ought never
to tremble. And yet it trembles, today, its order makes something tremble.

As for swapping one's tunic with a woman, who can be sure of never having
been "in abomination"? Not me, I fear.

A number with the power of the infinite, the number of recommendations
concerning the corners and holes of the tallith, the tears, the edges, the hems, the
knotting and unknotting of the fringes: we'd need pages, volumes, impossible and
interminable analysis because every analysis, every untying of the threads must
first appear before their law. Before the orders they give, for it is a gift they order
[*c'est un don qu'ils ordonnent*]. The big tallith, mine, the one I've already spoken
about, one wraps oneself in it during prayer. I think I haven't worn mine for almost half a century. And I do not know what it is made of. But it is there.
Tangible and close, even though in order to get on with each other we never speak
to each other. When as a young man I did sometimes wear it, I was always care-
ful to unfold its greatest surface, amply. I never imitated those who sometimes
roll it round their neck like a white woolen scarf.

Before wrapping oneself up in the tallith, at the moment of saying the blessing, which one must do standing up and taking care that the fringes do not drag

on the ground (in which case they must be picked up and can, it is said, be placed in the belt), one must examine not only the fringes but also the threads in the holes and the twists. It is above all necessary to analyze, undo knots, separate threads, prevent them from sticking to each other. On one condition: that it not delay the prayer. Because one must never pray too late or *à contretemps*, that is, if I understand aright, alone, praying alone, absolutely alone—as apparently I've always done, but that's doubtless merely a superficial appearance. Here's what is prescribed in the *Kitsour Choul'hane Aroukh*, this black, all black book my father left me: "If one arrives late at the synagogue such that separating the fringes and examining them would prevent one from praying with the community, one does not need to examine them and separate them." Categorical imperative, then: don't be late. At all events not for prayer. You don't keep a prayer waiting, what's more it never lets itself be waited for, it comes before everything, before the order, before the question, before the reply, before dialogue, before knowledge, before the "this is" or the "what is... ?" it is neither true nor false, as a Greek philosopher even said. Even a Greek knew that! This is how I try to calculate the formidable time, the time of the verdict awaiting me, to be on time on time [*pour être à l'heure à l'heure*], but the "too late," "so late," the evening of the verdict remains so internal to it that I despair of ever effacing it, *sero te amavi*.

I do not know what my tallith is made of, I was saying, especially not of what substance, natural or artificial. It can be touched, but touch does not allow me to conclude. According to the Torah and the "works of the deciders," it would seem that wool is required.

"Wool": that's what the cloth should be made of, an animal tissue, then, and only yesterday, at the origin, a living tissue.

"Linen": this is permitted, at a pinch, but only when wool is lacking and it is

67

impossible to do otherwise. In that case, as we have seen, the fringes must be woolen and sewn onto leather, an animal skin, then, only yesterday, at the origin, that living skin the four corners are made of.

As for "silk" (be it "natural" or "artificial"), the duties are even more tangled. For we must distinguish the warp from the woof. For if the woof of the tallith is, as it should be, made of wool, whereas the warp is of cotton, silk, or "something similar," or vice versa, if the warp is made of wool whereas the woof is made of a textile (in the strict sense), silk or cotton, then, in these two cases, he who fears God will not bless such a tallith. For they say that woolen fringes only free you from this prescription for one sort of cloth. What appears to matter, after wool, after animality, is therefore the *homogeneity* of the textile (in the broad sense). When a silken tallith has woolen fringes, one will not bless it. In such a case, you have first to wrap it in another tallith, a woolen tallith, bless it, then wrap oneself in one's own silken tallith. But, homogeneity again, if the fringes are also of silk, like the tallith itself, the blessing is permitted. My *Kitsour Choul'hane Aroukh* specifies in brackets: "Silken tzitzith (fringes) are not common in our provinces, for the tzitziths must be spun with a view to what they are to be used for." The worst case, it's clear, is mixing wool and silk in the tzitzith.

As for the sewing of the corners and the threads themselves, that would be another book. To the contrary of what is imposed on the rest of the tallith, and especially its fringes, here rules the law of *heterogeneity* or dissimilarity: silken thread (or similar) for a linen tallith; for a silken tallith, however, avoid silken thread, and for a woolen tallith avoid woolen thread. Same thing for the hem around the hole. But that's true only if it's sewn with white thread, for "with colored thread," affirms the same text, "there is nothing to fear."

Have I insisted sufficiently on what matters to me here, that is, the living creature? What in the first place is commanded by the categorical imperative of wool and leather? Fur and skin: the tallith must be something living taken from something living worn by something living. But, more precisely and later, taken from something dead which was one day living, and burying the dead that was one day living. Living, that is something that will have had some relation to itself [*à soi*]. The living is the possibility of auto-affection, of time and delay: what, in self-affection, will have been able to touch itself.

—That's twice you've spoken of categorical imperative: just now you had not to be late (*sero*), now it's the law of skin, the law of the living...

—That may be the same thing, and I'm just saying why I hold these two imperatives to be untenable (but you know how important I think the untenable is: it's the very possibility of the promise, which must be able to be untenable and threatening, contrary to what they say). Here are the hypotheses or daydreams I'm offering. The imperative of fur, wool, and skin seems indeed to mean that, unlike veil, sail, or canvas, a tallith is primarily animal. Like the tefillin: a skin on skin. As the skin comes not from just any animal but from sheep, ewe or ram, it in some sense commemorates an experience one would call sacrificial if the word "sacrifice" were not a bad translation for *Korban* ("approach," "coming together") and a translation that moreover takes us back toward the cultures of the veil. So a living creature wears something living, a living creature wraps up, until death,[12] in what was something living offered to something living, a mortal wraps up in what will have been living and put to death by its own, as a sacrifice—or rather as what gets translated as sacrifice. If there is a "truth" of this shawl, it depends less on the lifting or the unfolding of a veil, on some unveiling or revelation, than on the unique event, the gift of the law and the "coming together" it calls back to itself. Even if one translates this gift of the Law as Revelation, the figure of the veil, the intuition and the movement of vision count for less than the taking-place of the event, the singular effectivity of the "once only" as history of the unique: the time, the trace of the date, and the date itself as trace.

I continue to murmur, under the protection of hypothesis: when prayer tends to replace, in "coming together," the bloody sacrifice and the putting to death of the living creature, then the prayer shawl, the tallith, and the tzitzith commemorate both the privileged animal of the sacrifice—the wool of sheep or ram, the leather, etc.,—*and*, leaping with one wingbeat to the eschatalogical term of the story, the sacrifice of sacrifice, the end of sacrifice in coming together, its unterminated and perhaps interminable sublimation, the coming together of the infinite coming together in the orison of prayer. (Following a suggestion of Maimonides, God himself preferred mankind not to end in one go the murderous sacrifice[13] and it's true it's taking a long time—how long, my God...) We'd still need to find out, if we held to this hypothesis, where to inscribe a circumcision in this history of the tallith. Is it still a "sacrifice," a "coming together," and the attenuation, the delay, the infinite moratorium on crueler mutilations? I'm thinking of all those cloths that are wrapped round the penis of the baby circumcised on the eighth day, of that sort of shroud too, all bloody, in which the removed piece of flesh might be buried. Detached skin, but assumed (taken from oneself, alliance of floating skin, a scarf or a muffler), the tallith hangs on the body like a memory of circumcision. A circumcision reserved for the man, this one too. Basically it is the same thing, the same, and being-oneself. Ordered to the given order of the other, himself. *Ipse*, the power itself, and the law, the law of the father, of the son, of the brother or the husband, the laws of hospitality

70

(*hospes, hosti-pet-s, posis, despotes, utpote, ipse*, etc., the "mysterious *-pse* of *ipse*," says Benveniste, naively astonished[14]).

But never. Up to the end, never, whatever may happen: in no case, whatever the verdict at the end of so formidable a journey,[15] never can one get rid of a tallith. One must never, ever, at any moment, throw it away or reject it. One must especially not ill-treat the fringes, even if they have become useless: "Some people are so meticulous as to keep them in a book and make bookmarks of them: since they have served once to accomplish a commandment, may another commandment be accomplished with them."[16]

Which is what I am doing here, basically, and signing and booking and dating,[17] as always, *à contretemps*.

3

São Paulo, December 4–8, 1995

Von Querah
komm ein, als die Nacht
das Notsegel
bauscht sich. . . .

Paul Celan

Indirectly
Come, by night, to
the sail of distress
is filling. . . .

Das seidenverhangene Nirgend
widmet dem Strahl seine Dauer,
ich kann dich hier
sehn.

Paul Celan

The silk-hung nowhere
Dedicates its duration to the ray,
here I can
see you

→ **Have I managed to demonstrate it? What separates the logic or topic of the veil from those of the shawl,** that shawl called tallith, this tallith unique up to and including the number of its corners, wings, fringes, so many commandments, is the difference of the event, the irreducible reference to the One, to the One + n that multiplies only the first time and gives me my tallith, my own, to me alone, both as order and as gift, whereas I can and must never reappropriate it for myself, assigning myself thus my ipseity in what we really must call a history, a single history. The uniqueness of this reference, the untranslatable carry of this ference prevents a tallith, which one cannot and must not get rid of, from being or becoming, like every veil, merely a figure, a symbol, a trope.

Does this mean that the literality of "tallith," my tallith, is irreducible?

How to avoid hearing even here, in the name of this city, the *Epistle to the Romans*? Its author thought he knew the literality of the letter. He prided himself on being able to distinguish, for the first time, he no doubt thought, wrongly, the circumcision of the heart, according to the breath and the spirit, from the circumcision of body or flesh, circumcision "according to the letter."[1]

In the *Epistle to the Corinthians*, the same Paul (my young dead brother, dead before my birth, was also called Paul, Paul Moses), the same one who attacked the literal circumcision of men, that same one wanted to veil woman and un-veil man. During prayer or the prophetic act.

He writes in his letter: "the head of every man, is messiah;/the head of woman, is man; the head of the messiah, is Elohim./Any man who prays or transmits his inspiration head covered [*pas aner proseukhomenos e propheteuon kata kephales ekhon . . . omnis vir orans, aut prophetans velato capite*] dishonors his head./Every woman who prays or transmits her inspiration head uncovered/dishonors her head, yes, as though she were shaven./If then the woman is not veiled, let her also shave herself! /But if it is shameful for a woman to be shorn or shaved,/let her veil herself! /For the man is not obliged to veil his head:/he is the image and the glory of Elohim;/Woman is the glory of man./For man was not drawn from woman,/but woman comes from man./Man was not created for woman,/but woman for man./So the woman must have on her head a power [an insignium of power, a sign of authority, *potestatem, exousiam*],/because of the messengers."[2]

And this very mild, this terrible Paul dares, for he dares with all the daring whose monstrous progeny are our history and culture (see the erections of São Paulo the proud), this Paul who preferred a good Greek to a bad Jew, this Paul who claimed to know literally what is the breath of spirit and teach it to the Jew so that he would become a good Jew, better than the good Greek, this Paul dares to leave us to judge, he dares to say, to say to us (Jews or Greeks?) that he leaves us to judge. He goes so far as to invoke again, like so many others closer to us, both Rosenzweig and Freud, for example, Nature, Nature herself (*e physis aute, ipsa natura*), he turns us toward it at the moment he lets us judge: "Judge for yourselves [*En umin autois krinate, vos ipsi judicate*]:/is it appropriate for a woman to pray to Elohim unveiled?/Does not nature herself teach us/that it is a dishonor for the man to have long hair?/But the woman who wears long hair, that's a glory for her,/for her hair was given her as adornment."[3]

—Your epistle against Saint Paul is double-edged, like what you say about circumcision. In everything you're suggesting, with little airs of elliptical reticence, it's as though you were against circumcision but also against those who are against circumcision, you ought to make your mind up. You're against everything... Like what you say against the veil, in your Penelopean discourse, make your mind up... Make your mind up and develop a coherent comparatist hypothesis, with as its key a politics of the tallith, of the veil, the *chador* or the *kipa* in a secular and democratic school system... [4]

—Not in a hurry. Yes, I'm against, yes, yes I am. Against those who prescribe the veil and other such things, against those who forbid it too, and who think they can forbid it, imagining that this is good, that it is possible and that it is meaningful. Not in a hurry: the scholarly, the secular, and the democratic belong through and through to cultures of the tallith and the veil, etc., people don't even realize any longer... Contamination is everywhere. And we hadn't finished, I haven't finished with Saint Paul. The one who wanted to veil the heads of the women and unveil those of the men, that very one denounced Moses and the children of Israel. He accused them of having given in to the veil, of not having known how to lift the veil, the veil over the face of God, the veil over the covenant, the veil on the heart.

The Messiah, the Man-God and the two Resurrections, *voilà* the great Unveiler. Perhaps it's because of that, that at his death the veil of the temple tore. After having recalled that the "service of death, engraved in letters on stones," "was in such glory that the B'nai Israel were unable to fix their eyes on the face of Moshe because of the glory of his face, ephemeral however,"[5] Saint Paul wonders how the service of the breath or the spirit (therefore of life and not of death) would not be still more glorious, more luminous. And this light is *unveiling*:

> Having such a hope, we employ a full frankness;/but not like Moshe putting a veil over his face/so that the B'nai Israel could not stare at the end of the ephemeral . . . /But their thoughts hardened. For up to the present day/the same veil remains, on reading the antique pact./It is not unveiled [*idipsum velamen in lectione veteris testamenti manet non revelatum, to auto kalumma epi te anagnosei tes palaias daithekes menei*], for it is in the Messiah that he disappears./But still today, when Moshe is read, a veil lies on their heart./It is when he turns toward the Adôn that the veil is removed. . . . But if our announcement is veiled, it is for the lost ones that it is veiled,/those whose thoughts the Elohim of that era blinded.[6]

→ **Un-veiled *Savoir* of language beyond language**, of the french-language when it overtakes the french-language. For notwithstanding what we said above about the untranslatable, it would be naive to suppose that *Savoir* can be read only "in French," in the French language such *in fact* as it is given. You have to know what she does to the French language. *Savoir* will be read only in a French to come, whether it recognizes itself therein or not, and this can only happen *in delayed form*. Whence this inimitable gesture consisting in inheriting without inheriting, reinventing mother and father. *Savoir* gives the language the advance of an unpickable and unprecedented tunic, almost invulnerable (it has not to be so absolutely), unique, hard-wearing through the supple and tight weaving of all the given threads. No doubt the form and the meaning hold together in the same sewing, indissociably, in the weaving of one and the same text, a poem without example. But this one holds, it holds to itself by holding to what has happened, holds onto it and holds itself onto it by virtue of an operation of writing that indebts itself to a "real" operation, "in the world," right on one body: ference or reference of a one-off. Through the carry [*portée*], the graciously carried grace of this ference, *Savoir* indebts itself, recognizing its debt, to an event that remains unique, forever unique, forever heterogeneous to every language, that is, the operation that gave her her sight back, one day, not long ago, to herself, the signatory of *Savoir*, in one go, through the armed hand of the other, armed with a laser forever depriving her forever of the unseen.

—When you refer thus to the irreducible reality of an event (outside discourse but not outside text), I am really worried. It looks so unlike you, you look so unlike yourself, it looks so unlike the image of you that circulates in these regions. It's as though you were talking about the scenario for a soap in which (as happens) you have to change a character because the actor died or broke his contract.

—You mustn't believe in images, especially not when they circulate "in these regions." Above all you have to wonder what other image, what other, and what other of the image is being forbidden in that case. One is only astonished if one has not yet thought through the strange event nicknamed *signature*. It is auto-hetero-referential. Why must one say, in all rigor, as I have just done, "the signatory" of *Savoir*? In order to analyze a sort of hem: on the edge where it stands,

the signature does not belong simply within the cloth on the edge of which it is sewn. It will remain forever heterogeneous to it even if, however, it is not external to it, any more than the date. We have already verified this fact, and we could repeat this verification almost infinitely with so many texts by the same author, other sentences, other poems. They could have the same meaning ("at last I see, miracle," etc.), be so alike as to be mistakable for each other as to their form, but what *Savoir* says, referring directly to it, by its date, its signature, I can, as can others, know it *elsewhere*, thanks to other witnesses, other words given. Although they overflow *Savoir*, these attestations nonetheless form a text, traces, an in-finite corpus. They attest that the eye operation, sight returned, the "miracle," the "giving," took place only once in "reality." That "reality" exceeds *Savoir* but that excess remains caught, even as an overlap, a hem, or the tear they suture, in the poetic stitching of an experience that could announce it in the same words of the same language. Whence the effects of anticipated iterability we have pointed out.

Each time it's like that, the operation of this operation, the operation of poetic writing. Indebting itself to the other operation, the so-called "real" operation, it also indebts itself to the other's operation, that event that happens where I am no longer operating, where I am operated. Which does not mean that the hand of the other knows what it's doing, and that knowledge belongs to the other. An accident is always possible, as we have said, it has even taken place and catastrophe was avoided at the last minute, through strikes and traffic jams. Each time this unheard-of operation operates in this way, thus and otherwise, in each text signed by Hélène Cixous, in her opus that is also the body proper of her corpus, but a body proper exposed, vulnerable, expropriable in advance: readable unreadable. Vulnerable: an almost invulnerable tunic, we were saying, and it must not be absolutely invulnerable, such is the condition of the signature. I sign, an

"I" signs, she signs always in the very place of the wound, in the place of the wound that is only possible, of course, but so virtual that it remains, the possible wound is assigned, it bears the bereaved memory of an unrefusable lesion: you'd think it was older than self, you can have forgotten it but it carries on dictating the place of all the blows to which we are sensitive, all the blows of fate we await and fear as though we necessarily desired even the worst of them. That explains in part, surprise or not, that the reading of what happens thus, through *this* corpus *here*, to the french-language, to its in-self-out-of-self ipseity, to the putting-outside-self of its being-in-self, that that very thing remains to come in the French of the France of this century. I know of no more perverse and unjust misprision. But I do not foresee the future thus promised, I foretell it. Foretelling it, I do not describe a next day that will be, as if in advance one were lifting a veil to allow the predictable future to be seen, a being to come that one would see coming. No, the gage of my foretelling *destines*. It calls to make come, it destines itself here differently: beyond any truth as onto-logical revelation. It destines itself to those men or women who will know how to read, of course. But knowing how to read here, *voilà* the circle, is learned only on the basis of the gage given, and given in the first instance to what it's a question of *reading finally*, equal to [*à la hauteur de*] what *you have to read*: this corpus that is given to you, not this corpus finally un-veiled, but this corpus that has undone itself from the veil, this corpus that has known, from the operation of the other, how to undo itself from veiling and from unveiling. That is [*à savoir*], to reply about the veil: to Saint Paul as much as to Saint Freud, as to the same. (But Paul remains, and Freud.) For this to happen, equal to this corpus, the corpus thus disenveiled, you have to write and sign in turn, countersign in writing something else, in another language, without betraying the injunction or the call of the first seal. One will never be able to *prove* that it happened, but only *swear* that it did. Perjury *must* remain possible. That's a duty that must be respected.

→ **Of man and woman: the tallith is proper to man, like circumcision.** As for knowing whether some discourse on fetishism...

—Haven't you exhausted them, as you claim?

—It's true, but I would still like to know if a "theory-of-fetishism" could ever measure up to the infinite tenderness that can be inspired, on contact, on caressing, by a tallith, mine, and every "my own tallith" (as if some "my own tallith" preceded ipseity and the ability to say "I"). I would like to sing the very solitary softness of my tallith, softness softer than softness, entirely singular, both sensory and non-sensory, calm, acquiescent, a stranger to anything maudlin, to effusion or to pathos, in a word to all "Passion." And yet, compassion without limit, compassion without idolatry, proximity and infinite distance. I love the peaceful passion, the distracted love my tallith inspires in me, I get the impression it allows me that distraction because it is sure, so sure of me, so little worried by my infidelities. It does not believe in my inconstancies, they do not affect it. I love it and bless it with a strange indifference, my tallith, in a familiarity without name or age. As if faith and knowledge, another faith and another knowledge, a knowledge without truth and without revelation, were woven together in the memory of an event to come, the absolute delay of the verdict, of a verdict to be rendered and which is, was, or will make itself arrive without the glory of a luminous vision. My white tallith belongs to the night, the absolute night. You will never know anything about it, and no doubt neither will I.

And yet, of course, it will not suffice to profess that a theoretical knowledge about the truth of fetishism here reveals itself or turns out to be impotent—and that a "my own tallith" will always remain incommensurable with it. One will always be able to take the tallith for a fetish, on condition of an upheaval in the axioms of the theorem of restricted fetishism and a formalization—I attempted it in *Glas* and elsewhere—of generalized fetishism. At the moment of the verdict, this theory would no longer be merely a theory, it would take into account, at the end of the day, with the whole history engaged in it (from Exodus to Saint Paul to Freud to everything that is implied and placed *en abyme* in *A Silkworm Of One's Own*), this thought of the event without truth unveiled or revealed, without phallogocentrism of the greco-judeo-paulino-islamo-freudo-heideggeriano-lacanian veil, without phallophoria, that is, without procession or theory of the phallus, without veiling-unveiling of the phallus, or even of the mere place, strictly hemmed in, of the phallus, living or dead. This culpable edging of the phallus, the edges of this cut that support the veil and hold it out like a tent or an awning, a roof, a canvas, this theoretical toilet of the phallus is none other than the concept, yes, the concept in itself, the possibility of the concept, of the concept in itself. The phallus is the concept, you can't oppose it, any more than you can oppose a "sexual theory." Unless you do something different, you can only oppose to it another concept or another theory, a knowledge like another. Very little. It is not enough to have concepts at one's disposal, you have to know how to set them, like one sets sails, often to save oneself of course, but on condition of knowing how to catch the wind in one's sails: a question of force, concepts and veils are there only in view of this question of force. All I'm doing here, they'd say, is citing Benjamin: "What matters for the dialectician is to have the wind of world history in his sails [*den Wind der Weltgeschichte in den Segeln zu haben*]. Thinking means for him: setting the sails [*Denken heisst bei ihm, Segel setzen*]. What is important is how they are set. Words are his sails [*Worte sind seine Segel*: unless one translates also, "his sails are (merely) words"]. The way they are set makes them into concepts. . . . Being a dialectician means having the wind of history in one's sails. The sails are the concepts [*Die Segel sind die Begriffe*]. It is not enough to have sails at one's disposal [*über die Segel zu verfügen*]. What is decisive is knowing the art of setting them [*die Kunst, sie setzen zu können*]."[7]

What knowledge does not know is what happens. *Voilà* what happens. For what happens (the operation I don't operate, the one that operates me), you must *Savoir*, another *Savoir*, here it is, the other's.

→ **Abyss and gap in memory, ripening** [*véraison*]: all that goes before has not been dreamed, it is the narrative of a true dream I've only just woken from. A "bad" dream, enough to make you thrash about like a wounded devil in an invisible straitjacket, when you can't stop crumpling the sheets around you to make a hole in the violence and find the way out. Far from Europe, from one ocean to another, over the Cordillera de los Andes, weeks of hallucinatory travel during which I was dreaming of the interruption of the dream, the sentence of life or death, the final whistle blown by a verdict that never stopped suspending its moratorium and stretching out its imminence. It has not yet taken place but I am almost awake. I am writing with a view to waking up and the better to prepare myself for the reality of the verdict, or better, for the verdict when it will have become reality itself, that is severity without appeal. But also without truth, or veracity, or veridicity, without the slightest promised reappropriation. Of course, I still dream of resurrection. But the resurrection I dream of, for my part, at the ends of the verdict, the resurrection I'm stretched out toward, would no longer have to be a miracle, but the reality of the real, quite simply, if it's possible, ordinary reality finally rendered, beyond fantasy or hallucination. The weaving machine comes to a stop, unexpectedly, the bobbin comes to rest between dream and reality, but in a now unrecognizable silence, without the slightest image still. The interruption of the dream will always remain improbable, like the end of the journey I'm still flying toward. But the duration counts, and the endurance of the voyage, the return flight. Already I'm getting ready. I am ready, I say to myself, I'm quite close to enjoying in peace, I'm already enjoying the turbulence and the burst cloud, the accepted self-evidence, the new finitude affirmed. What luck, this verdict, what feared chance: yes, now, there will be for me worse than death, I would never have believed it, and the enjoyment here nicknamed "resurrection," that is, the price to pay for the extraordinarily ordinary life toward which I should like to turn, without conversion, for some time still—such an enjoyment will be worth more than life itself.

Everything had begun the night before. I had just read *Savoir*. And before closing my eyes to give in to sleep, I let myself be invaded, as they say, gently, in gentleness, by a childhood memory, a true childhood memory, the opposite of a dream, and here I embroider no longer:

Before I was thirteen, before ever having worn a tallith and having even dreamed of possessing my own, I cultivated (what's the link?) silkworms, the caterpillars or larvae of the bombyx. *I now discover that that's called sericulture (from Seres, the Seres, it appears, a people of Eastern India with whom there was a silk trade). In the four corners of a shoebox, then, I'd been shown how, I kept and fed silkworms. Every day, but I would have liked to make myself the indefatigable officiant of this service. Several times a day, the same liturgy, you had to offer them mulberry leaves, these little indifferent idols. For weeks, I would leave the room where the box was kept only to look for mulberry trees. These trips were journeys and adventure: we didn't know where to look for them anymore, or whether we were going to find any more. My silkworms stayed there, then, with me, in my place as in their place, in the rack of the* magnanery, *so many words I knew nothing of in those days. In truth, they needed lots of mulberry, too much, always too much, these voracious little creatures. They were especially voracious between moltings (at the moment called the* instar*). You could hardly see the mouths of these white or slightly grayish caterpillars, but you could sense they were impatient to nourish their secretion. Through their four moltings, the caterpillars, every one for itself, were themselves, in themselves, for themselves, only the time of a passage. They were animated only in view of the transformation of the mulberry into silk. We would sometimes say the worm, sometimes the caterpillar. I would observe the progress of the weaving, of course, but basically without seeing anything. Like the movement of this production, like this becoming-silk of a silk I would never have believed natural, as this extraordinary process remained basically invisible, I was above all struck by the impossible embodied in these little creatures in their shoebox. It was not impossible, of course, to distinguish between a head and a tail, and so, virtually, to see the difference between a part and a whole, and to find some sense in the thing, a direction, an orientation. But it was impossible to discern a sex. There was indeed something like a brown mouth but you could not recognize in it the orifice you had to imagine to be at the origin of their silk, this milk become thread, this filament prolonging their body and remaining attached to it for a certain length of time: the* *extruded saliva of a very fine sperm, shiny, gleaming, the miracle of a feminine ejaculation, which would catch the light and which I drank in with my eyes. But basically without seeing anything. The silk-producing glands of the caterpillar can, I've just learned, be labial or salivary, but also rectal. And then it was impossible to distinguish between several states, between several movements, between several self-affections of the same miniscule living spontaneity. The self-displacement of this little fantasy of a penis, was it erection or detumescence? I would observe the invisible progress of the weaving, a little as though I were about to stumble on the secret of a marvel, the secret of this secret over there, at the infinite distance of the animal, of this little innocent member, so foreign yet so close in its incalculable distance. I cannot say that I appropriated the operation, nor will I say anything other or the contrary. What I appropriated for myself without turning it back on myself, what I appropriated for myself over there, afar off, was the operation, the operation through which the worm itself secreted its secretion. It secreted it, the secretion. It secreted. Intransitively. It dribbled. It secreted absolutely, it secreted a thing that would never be an object to it, an object for it, an object it would stand over against. It did not separate itself from its work. The silkworm produced outside itself, before itself, what would never leave it, a thing that was no other than itself, a thing that was not a thing, a thing that belonged to it, to whom it was properly due. It projected outside what proceeded from it and remained at bottom at the bottom* of it: *outside itself in itself and near itself, with a view to enveloping it soon entirely. Its work and its being toward death. The living, tiny but still divisible formula of absolute knowledge. Absolute nature and culture. Sericulture was not man's thing, not a thing belonging to the man raising his silkworms. It was the culture of the silkworm* qua *silkworm. Secretion of what was neither a veil, nor a web (nothing to do with the spider), nor a sheet nor a tent, nor a white scarf, this little silent finite life was doing nothing other, over there, so close,*

89

right next to me but at an infinite distance, nothing other than this: preparing itself to hide itself, liking to hide itself, with a view to coming out and losing itself, spitting out the very thing the body took possession of again to inhabit it, wrapping itself in white night. With a view to returning to itself, to have for oneself what one is, to have oneself [s'avoir] *and to be oneself* [s'être] *while ripening but dying thus at birth, fainting to the bottom of oneself, which comes down to burying oneself gloriously in the shadow at the bottom of the other: "Aschenglorie: . . . grub ich mich in dich und in dich." Love itself. Love made itself make love right next to the watching dreaming child. For the child could not believe what he was seeing, he could not see what he thought he was seeing, he was already telling himself a story, this story, like a philosophy of nature for a shoebox (romanticism in Algeria, in the middle of summer— for I was forgetting to say that, by its essence, all this could only have been possible, in my memory in any case, in summer, in the heat of the holidays in El-Biar), namely that the silkworm buried itself, came back to itself in its odyssey, in a sort of absolute knowledge, as if it had to wrap itself in its own shroud, the white shroud of its own skin, in order to remain with itself, the being it had been with a view to re-engendering itself in the spinning of its filiation, sons or daughters—beyond any sexual difference or rather any duality of the sexes, and even beyond any coupling. In the beginning, there was the worm that was and was not a sex, the child could see it clearly, a sex perhaps but which one? His bestiary was starting up. This philosophy of nature was for him, for the child I was but that I remain still, naiveté itself, doubtless, but also the time of infinite apprenticeship, the culture of the rag trade, culture made up according to fiction, the autobiography of the lure,* Dichtung und Wahrheit, *a novel of education, a novel of sericulture that he was beginning to write with a view to addressing it to himself, to stand up in it himself in a Sabbath of colors and words: the word* mulberry *was never far from ripening and dying* [mûrir. . . mourir] *in him, the green of the mulberry whose green color he warded off like everyone in the family, a whole history and war of religions, he cultivated it like a language, a phoneme, a word, a verb (green [vert] itself, and greenery [verdure], and going green [verdir], and worm [ver] and verse [vers] and glass [verre] and rod [verge] and truth [vérité], veracious or veridical [vérace ou véridique], perverse and virtue [pervers et vertu], all the crawling bits of words with ver- in even greater number, that he will celebrate later and recalls here, one more time, without veil or shame.*[8]

*(*Virus *belongs in his imagination to the same family, it's a little perverse and pernicious worm* [un petit ver pervers et pernicieux], *neither living nor dead, which carries delayed death in its self-multiplication. It is also, moreover, a slime from slugs, in Latin, and for Virgil or Pliny the seed of animals, for Cicero a venom or a poison.)*

Just now I've found the most beautiful of them, which was looking for me from the start: **véraison**. *Véraison (from* vérir, varire, *"to vary, change color") is the moment of ripening, the moment of maturation. Fruits, especially fruits of the vine, begin then to take on the color they will have when they reach maturity. The berry starts to grow again, the grape becomes translucent in white vines, red in black vines.*

Now long after the formation of the cocoon, an incalculable time for the child, a time without common measure, when the damp patch would finally appear, when an unknown blood, a red almost black, came from within to soften and penetrate the skin, then open the way for the moth's wings, at this moment of awakening as much as of birth, at the moment at which the unforeseeable reappropriation took place, the return to itself of the silkworm, which lets fall its old body like a bark with holes in it, what happened then, what in truth, I must tell you, happened once, once only, the véraison in the blinking of an eye, the grain of a telephone ring, that one and only

91

time, like the surprise I had to expect, for it never makes a mistake, never misleads me, that véraison that took place only once but will demand all the time given to become what it was, I will never tell you that tale.

I have promised.

A lapse of time: it was only an interval, almost nothing, the infinite diminution of a musical interval, and what a note, what news, what music. The verdict. As if suddenly evil never, nothing evil ever, happened again. As though evil would only happen again with death—or only later, too late, so much later.

Notes

[Translator's note:] The title and subtitle of the piece already introduce a number of more or less untranslatable motifs that will run throughout the text. The title, *Un ver à soie*, literally means "A silkworm," but the play on *soi* (oneself) is important (as in *Une chambre à soi*, "A Room of One's Own"). The subtitle, *Points de vue piqués sur l'autre voile*, is more difficult. *Points de vue* more or less corresponds to the English "Points of View," but *points* is also the term for a "stitch," and, aurally, runs into *point de vue* where the *point* can be a mildly old-fashioned intensifier of *pas* (not). Thus, given the developments to come in the text, *point de vue* could reasonably be taken as "no view at all." *Piquer* here most obviously means "to stitch," but carries an overtone of its colloquial meaning, "to steal, to pinch"; and *voile* could here be either masculine (veil), or feminine (sail). In this context, the frequent use of *voilà*, "there," "see" (from *vois là*, "see there," but homophonous with *voile à . . .* , "(a) veil on") has seemed worth signaling by keeping the word in French. To the translator's relief and despair, some of these possibilities and difficulties are later explicitly discussed in the text, along with their untranslatability.

93

This translation originally appeared in *Oxford Literary Review* 18 (1997): 3–63.

A Silkworm of One's Own, Chapter 1

1. [Translator's note:] *Odyssey*, 2.96–104. Trans. E. V. Rieu (Harmondsworth: Penguin, 1946), pp. 39–40. Penelope's speech here is in fact being reported to the Assembly at Ithaca by Antinous, the leader of the Suitors.

2. [Translator's note:] *Savoir*, "to know"; *s'avoir*, "to have or possess oneself."

3. "Kai idou to katapetasma tou naou eskhisthe [ap'] anothen eos kato eis duo . . . Et ecce velum templi scissum est in duas partes a summo usque deorsum" (Matthew 27:51); "tout heliou eklipontos . . . eskhisthe de to katapetasma tou naou meson . . . Et obscuratus est sol; et velum templi scissum est medium . . . " (Luke 23:45); "Kai to katapetasma tou naou eskhisthe eis duo ap'anothen eos kato . . . Et velum templi scissum est in duo, a summo usque deorsum" (Mark 15:38).

4. Exodus 26:31.

5. We would need to cite more than one translation. Some oppose "veil" to "curtain" (A. Chouraqui, *Noms*, Desclée de Brouwer; Louis Segond, Nouvelle édition de Genève, 1979, Société biblique de Genève), the other distinguishes "curtain" (instead of "veil") from "drape" (E. Dhorme, in the Bibliothèque de la Pléiade). [The Authorized translation has "vail" and "hanging"; the New Revised version has "curtain" and "screen."—Trans.] In the case of the first veil or first curtain, we're dealing with the work of an *artist* or an *inventor*; the second (curtain or drape) is merely the work of an *embroiderer*: "work of embroidery," "embroiderer's work." The difference appears to be clearly made [though perhaps less so in the English translations: the Authorized version is less clear: "And thou shalt make a vail of blue, and purple, and scarlet, and fine twined linen of cunning work: with cherubims shall it be made" (26:31); "And thou shalt make an hanging for the door of the tent, of blue, and purple, and scarlet, with fine twined linen, wrought with needlework" (26:36). The New Revised Edition has "You shall make a curtain of blue, purple, and crimson yarns, and of fine, twisted

linen; it shall be made with cherubim skillfully worked into it" (26:31); "You shall make a screen for the entrance of the tent, of blue, purple, and crimson yarns, and of fine twisted linen, embroidered with needlework" (26:36)]. On the one hand, *art* and *inaugural invention*, on the other, a secondary know-how or technique. Two examples (italics mine [I have translated these French translations as literally as is feasible.—Trans.]):

"Make a *veil*:/azure, purple, scarlet cochenille,/byssus twist,/it will be an *inventor's* work: griffons./You will give it on four acacia columns,/covered with gold, their hooks of gold,/on four silver plinths. Give the veil, under the hooks, have come there, inside the veil,/the ark of testimony. And the veil will distinguish for you/*between the sanctuary and the sanctuary of sanctuaries*,/Give the *veil* on the ark of testimony,/in the *sanctuary of sanctuaries*./Place the table outside the *veil*,/and the candelabrum opposite the table, /on the wall of the dwelling, toward the South. Give the table on the wall to the North./Make a *curtain* for the opening of the tent:/azure, purple, scarlet cochenille,/byssus twist,/*embroiderer's* work . . . ." (Chouraqui: in a later edition, in 1985, the translation is substantially modified: "veil" is replaced now by "screen," now by "absolutory," "inventor" by "weaver.")

"You will also make the *Curtain* of violet purple and red purple, of scarlet vermilion and fine linen twist. It will be made [ornamented] with Cherubim, *artist's* work./You will place it on four acacia columns covered with gold, with golden hooks on four silver bases. You will place the *Curtain* under the hooks and there, within the *Curtain*, you will place the Ark of the Testimony. The *Curtain* will be for you the *separation between the holy and the Holy of Holies*./You will place the Propitiatory on the Ark of the testimony in the *Holy of Holies*./You will put the Table outside the *Curtain* and the Candelabrum opposite the Table on the side of the Dwelling to the South; you will place the Table on the north side./Then you will make a *Drape* at the entry of the Tent, of violet purple and red purple, in crimson vermilion and fine linen twist, *embroiderer's* work" (Dhorme).

6. Trans. A. Chouraqui. "And they will make me a sanctuary and I shall dwell in the midst of them" (Dhorme). "They will make me a sanctuary, and I shall live in their midst" (Segond).

7. [Editor's note by René Major for the French publication of this text in *Le contretemps*, 2 (1997):] The consequence of this is analyzed in *Glas* (Galilée, 1974 [trans. John P. Leavey, Jr., and Richard Rand, University of Nebraska Press, 1986]), for example around the following passage:

> But this place and this figure have a singular structure: the structure encloses its void within itself, shelters only its own interiorized desert. It opens onto nothing, encloses nothing, contains as its treasure only nothingness: a hole, an empty spacing, a death. A death or a dead man, because according to Hegel space is death and because this space is also one of absolute vacuity. Nothing behind the curtains. Hence the ingenuous surprise of the non-Jew when he opens, when he is allowed to open or when he violates the tabernacle, when he enters the dwelling or the temple and after so many ritual detours to reach the secret center, he discovers nothing—only nothingness.
>
> No center, no heart, an empty space, nothing.
>
> You undo the bands, move the cloths, pull back the veils, part the curtains: nothing but a black hole or a deep gaze, colorless, formless, and lifeless. This is the experience of the powerful Pompey at the end of his avid exploration: "If no form [*Gestalt*] was offered to sensibility [*Empfindung*], meditation and adoration of an invisible object had at least to be given a direction [*Richtung*] and a delimitation [*Ungrenzung*] enclosing that object—Moses gave them this in the form of the Holy of Holies of the Tabernacle, and subsequently the temple. Pompey was surprised when he got into the most inner place of the Temple, the center [*Mittelpunkt*] of adoration and there, at the root of the national spirit, in the hope of recognizing the living soul of this exceptional people at its center and perceiving a being [an essence, *Wesen*] offered to his meditation, something full of meaning [*Sinvolles*] offered to his respect, and when entering the secret [the familiar and secret intimacy, *Geheimnis*] before the ultimate spectacle he felt himself mystified [*getauscht*] and found what he was looking for in an empty space [*in einem leeren Raume*]" (p. 60 [pp. 49–50; trans. mod.]).

8. [Translator's note:] "*Deux relèves, donc, l'une ne relevant plus de l'autre mais parce qu'elle relève de l'autre, pour relever de l'autre. L'une se garde de l'autre.*" The first sentence plays across the noun *relève*, proposed by

Derrida to translate Hegel's *Aufhebung*, and the verb *relever de* (to belong to, to be a matter for, to come under). The formula *l'une se garde de l'autre*, used by Derrida in, for example, *Mal d'archive* (Paris: Galilée, 1995), 124–5, condenses *se garder de quelque chose* (to beware of something, to steer clear of something, to protect oneself against something, here the other), and *se garder quelque chose*, with the *de l'* now becoming a partitive article (to keep something for oneself, here to keep some other for oneself). "The one keeps the other (off)," perhaps. Here the feminine *l'une* refers to the *relève* mentioned earlier.

9. *Confessions*, 10:27, p. 38.

10. [Translator's note:] More improbable in French: *Je connais H.C.* (I know H.C.), but the present tense is maintained in *Je connais H.C. depuis 33 ans*, "I have known H.C. for 33 years."

11. [Translator's note:] *La révélation du jour*, also "The revelation of the (day)light."

12. For at least three reasons:

1. Because of the name *Lenz*, of course. Celan has it appear right at the start of *Gespräch im Gebirg*: "For the Jew, you know this well, what does he own that is really his, that is not lent, borrowed, never returned, went off then and came along, came from yonder on the road, the beautiful, incomparable road, went off, like Lenz, through the mountains, they'd let him live down below, where by force he belongs, in the depths, he, the Jew, went off and went off." [French translation by J. E. Jackson and A. du Bouchet, in *Strette* (Paris: Mercure de France, 1971), p. 171.]

2. Then because of the name *Klein*, another proper name immediately renamed by Celan and which was also that of Hélène Cixous's mother or grandfather. As if the name of Paul Celan had met the name of Hélène Cixous, following the poetic necessity of a time I do believe to be incontestable: "To meet him [i.e. Lenz] came his cousin . . . to meet the other, Gross came with Klein, and Klein, the Jew, made his stick silent before the stick of the Jew Gross."

3. Finally and above all, this story of cousins german (*Geschwisterkinder*) is also told as a story of eyes, weaving and veils: "But they,

cousins german, may the complaint reach back to God [*Gott sei's geklagt*], have no eyes [*keine Augen*]. Not, in truth, that they do not possess eyes, but in front there hangs a veil, not in front, no, behind, a moving veil [*ein beweglicher Schleier*]; scarcely has an image burst in than it remains suspended in the web [*im Geweb*], and a thread [*ein Faden*] is already in place, which weaves itself there [*der sich da spinnt*], around spins itself around the image, a veil thread [*ein Schleierfaden*]; itself weaves itself around, round the image, makes a child with it, half image and half veil [*halb Bild und halb Schleier*]" (ibid., p. 172).

13. [Translator's note:] *Sa laisse,* "her leash," but picking up the earlier play on the verb *laisser* (to let, to allow), and introducing the following development.

14. "Technics," the surgery of our time, my chances and my friends. None of this could have happened, happened to them or happened to me, only ten years ago. If Hélène Cixous got her sight back, I was able to dedicate to Jean-Luc Nancy, who inherited another heart, a text, *Touch,* still unpublished in French (trans. Peggy Kamuf in *Paragraph,* 16:2 [1993], 122–57). [And now cf. *Le toucher: Jean-Luc Nancy* (Paris: Galilée, 2000).—Trans.]

15. [Translator's note:] *Perdre son latin,* "not to be able to make head nor tail of something."

16. For example *Sein und Zeit,* p. 222 and passim [trans. Macquarrie and Robinson (Oxford: Blackwell, 1980), p. 265].

17. Ibid., p. 229 and *passim* [p. 272].

18. Complaint and accusation. *Klagen Anklagen.* I complain about myself to myself and I want, finally, to escape, that's my only excuse. Avowal, immodesty, and impudence. The fatigue of exhaustion is here the thing itself. It is identical with the very thing complained about. How can one complain about the thing itself? How can one lodge [*déposer*] such a complaint and hold the fatigue of exhaustion to be such a deposit? You have to *know* the thing itself, that thing thus called (the thing *itself, meisme,* with the phantasm of possiblity, the phantasm of power and possession lodged at the root, *metipse* of ipseity itself). But you have to *know,* too, and first, that the thing itself is always announced as what can stand behind the transparent, translucent, or opaque veil: the thing itself *behind* the veil or the thing it-

self the phantasm of which is itself an effect of the veil, as much as to say enveiled *thing* as *veiled cause*—of nudity, of modesty, of shame, of reticence (*Verhaltenheit*), of the law, of everything that hides and shows the sex, of the origin of culture and so-called humanity in general, in short of what links evil, radical evil, to *knowledge*, and knowledge to avowal, knowing-how-to-avow [*le savoir-avouer*] to knowledge avowed [*le savoir avoué*].

As the fatigue of exhaustion is here lodged, or lodges here its complaint against all this discourse, in truth against the matrix of this discourse, it owes it to itself to give up all modesty, to give up the most elementary politeness.

That's what allows me, in my great fatigue (great, believe me, you see), to refer to this or that of my still penelopean works those who want to see if I'm lying when I say I have already written too much on the veil, about it, thematically, inexhaustibly, and woven *right on* the veil, for example in all the texts on Heidegger, which is far from being insignificant here, in *Dissemination* (first in "Plato's Pharmacy," which begins with the *istos* or the tissue of the textile, and especially in "The Double Session," short treatise of the veil, the hymen, the wing, and the eyelid, etc., and short treatise written in "ver," that is, played according to the syllable, the vocable, or the letters "ver," the "ver" versified or vitrified, exhibited in a glass case in all its states), in *Spurs*, stuck in the "veils of all sorts," and in *Glas, La carte postale, D'un ton apocalyptique...*, *Mémoires d'aveugle*, etc. On what footing to make a fresh start, that's the question of this trip.

19. [Translator's note:] In English in the text.

20. [Translator's note:] See note 1 above.

21. [Translator's note:] "Commencer . . . à bien faire"; also alluding to the idiom "Ça commence à bien faire!" (It's getting a bit much).

22. Numbers 15:39. [Derrida here quotes the Dhorme translation, which I have rendered rather literally. The Authorized version has: "And it shall be unto you for a fringe, that ye may look upon it, and remember all the commandments of the LORD, and do them . . ."; the New Revised version, "You have the fringe so that, when you see it, you will remember all the commandments of the LORD and do them. . . ."—Trans.]

23. [Translations of the] translations by Segond and Chouraqui respectively.

24. "It is permitted to take occasionally the tallith of another to pray, even without his knowing it and to say the blessing for him, for in general it is admitted that people like the commandments to be accomplished with what remains to them, so long as it costs them nothing. But it must not be taken out of the house in which it is kept . . ." Rabbi Chlomoh Ganzfried, *Abrégé du Choul'han Aroukh*, trans. G. A. Guttel and L. Cohn, Libraire Colbo, Paris, 1966, vol. 1, p. 40.

25. Numbers 15:37–9: "And the LORD spake unto Moses, saying,/Speak unto the children of Israel, and bid them that they make them fringes in the borders of their garments through their generations, and that they put upon the fringe of the borders a riband of blue:/And it shall be unto you a fringe . . ." (Authorized version); "The LORD said to Moses:/Speak to the Israelites, and tell them to make fringes on the corners of their garments throughout their generations and to put a blue cord on the fringe at each corner./You have the fringe . . ." (New Revised). In the talmudic treatise *'Houlin* (88b and 89a), one can read: "What is more, Raba says: to recompense the saying of our father Abraham: 'That I will not take from a thread even to a shoelatchet . . .' (Genesis 14:23), Abraham obtained two commandments: that of the 'riband of blue . . .' (the *tzitzith*), and that of the 'band of *tephillin*' (phylacters). For it is said (Deuteronomy 28:10): 'And all the peoples shall see that the name of the Eternal is associated with yours,' and on this matter there is teaching: Rabbi Eliezer has said: 'They are [the phylacters] of the head.' But what about the 'riband of blue'? It is taught: Rabbi Meir has said: in what does blue differ from all colors? For blue is like the sea, and the sea like the firmament of the sky, and the firmament of the sky like sapphire, and sapphire like the throne of God, for it is said (Exodus 24:10): 'And they saw the God of Israel: and *there was* under his feet as it were a paved work of a sapphire stone . . . ,' and there is later (Ezechial, 1:26): 'there was the likeness of a throne, as the appearance of a sapphire stone. . . .'"

In his *Nouvelles Lectures Talmudiques*, which appeared a few days before his death, Levinas interrogates this passage, among others, to elaborate the question "Who is oneself?" what is the "self," the "oneself," the "*quant-à-soi*" (reserve)? (Paris: Minuit, 1995, pp. 77ff.).

A Silkworm of One's Own, Chapter 2

1. "It was *seeing-with-the naked-eye*, the miracle . . . and that was the miracle, giving. . . . And to think that this miracle was striking only her own . . . Quick, miracle! she was crying. Hold on! Slowly, miracle, she cried."

2. Pointing out only one occurrence of words in *V* that sometimes return, from beginning to end of *Savoir*, here's a simple cumulative list: *savoir, voile, voyait, pouvait, devant, aveu, vois, visage, venir, devrais, aveugle, devait, venait, suivant, arriver, privée, vit, invisible, vivante, voilà, ville, intervalle, avaient, voilette, pauvres, savait, mévoyait, vit, voir, vivre, réservait, vérités, découvertes, vain, vous, vîtes, saviez, gravement, rendez-vous, nouvelle, vaincre, l'invincible, vivant, vécu, caverne, venu, versé, veines, voici, avoir, pouvoir, devenir, avait, événement, vies, vu, vinrent, réserve, lèvent, lever, viens, visibles, vision, verre, vue, veille, lèvres, venait, voyante, violente, retrouver, équivalent, invu, invention, vie, avant, avez, vérité, visibilité, advenir, irréversible, vite, révoltait, vaines, veine, malvenue, dévoilée, envers, achever, délivré, vissements, vains, découvrait, avant, voyant, voyait, virginité, vivait, voyance, sauvée, savent, verrait, janvier, rives, bouleversait, reviendrait, révélée, levait, veut vouloir. . .* I may have missed some. But what is she fabricating in this fabric? What is she fabricating with these V's? Imagine someone wanting to translate them, translate their warp and their woof! Good luck and courage to this new royal weaver! For translation always fails when it gives up giving itself over to a certain alliance of lips and meaning, of palate and truth, of tongue to what it *does*, the unique poem.

Imagine too a parchment on which all the other words, the words without V have been burned, you reinvent them, you make other sentences, you want to *know* [*savoir*]. What has happened? What is happening? Nothing is impossible, and translation is not ruled out, but you need another economy for it, another poem. One could in this way deem a passage from *Messie* (Paris: Éditions des femmes, pp. 142ff.) to be a poetic translation of *Savoir*. Unless it's the other way round. It's another version, another poem, infinitely different and yet twin, almost contemporary, through the operation, the "miracle," and the mourning it names.

3. Hélène Cixous, *La* (Paris: Gallimard, 1976; rpt. Éditions des femmes, 1979).

4. Ibid., p. 132.

5. Ibid., p. 131.

6. Ibid., pp. 147–8; 193–4.

7. Ibid., p. 201.

8. Ibid., pp. 227–8.

9. [Translator's note:] A *voix voilée* is a husky voice.

10. From everywhere there comes upon her, in her language, pulled in by the very breath of the poem, a flotilla of black and white sails, black or white, black/white, a flotilla but always the same sail. For example, to cite only the most recent:

"Others, apart from me, really have died from a sail that was not white. The shirt you'd promised me you'd wear on Sunday should have been white, my love, and it was black. That was an error.

What? For a shirt? No, I swear not. No one can die from a shirt, nor even from a sail nor even from a letter. Dying from a sail is such a betrayal!" (*Beethoven à jamais ou l'existence de Dieu* [Paris: Éditions des femmes, 1993], pp. 24–5).

Or again, in the same book, the song of *Betrayal* (rendered innocent, if that were possible or necessary, by the sublimity of the silence or of the veiled avowal, by a keeping-silent that's able to speak or make understood without betraying):

"A brush of a finger—the sun goes down—Cut—Cut of faith—A finger. A word. A fake. An optical error. Instead of seeing one thinks one sees. And *voilà* the white black sail.

As for me, when I am betrayed, I do not know if I am betrayed by treachery or treason, or by myself. . . . I would never have believed that one day I would see as black the white sail between us" (Ibid., pp. 210–14). "A plane was passing, I flung myself into its belly, blood was running from my wings. . . . This is not a complaint. It is a confession: I indeed almost betrayed my love [. . .] No one will ever know. . . . The other:

'As soon as I saw you see me, I fled'" (Ibid., pp. 229–33).

11. Perhaps this is the place to situate an allusion of Emmanuel Levinas to this "trellis" of fringes through which a gaze would give itself over to God. After mentioning an irrectitude this time going "higher than rectitude" and leading, in separation, toward the He at the base of the You, Levinas notes, "Franz Rosenzweig interprets the *reply* given by Man to the Love with which God loves him, as the movement to one's neighbor. . . . This picks up the structure that rules a homelitic theme of Jewish thought: 'the fringes at the corners of clothes' the sight of which ought to recall to the faithful 'all the commandments of the Eternal' (Numbers 15:38–40), are called 'tz-itzith.' This word is linked, in the ancient rabbinic commentary called *Siphri,* to the verb 'tsouts,' one form of which, in the Song of Songs 2:9, means 'observe' or 'look': 'My true love . . . looks through the trellis.' The faithful looking at the 'fringes' that remind him of his obligations thus renders his gaze to the True Love observing him. And this would be the vis-à-vis or face to face with God!" *De Dieu qui vient à l'idée* (Paris: Vrin, 1982), p. 114 [*Of God Who Comes To Mind,* trans. Bettina Bergo (Stanford: Stanford University Press, 1998), p. 199n22].

12. I recalled this fact earlier: a tallith could become a shroud. But as I cannot help comparing (comparing, neither more nor less) the time of what I'm calling here the Verdict with the time of the "fearful days" between the New Year and the day of Expiation, as they are interpreted by Rosenzweig, I will be content to *quote* a passage from *The Star of Redemption,* merely to quote it whereas it ought to demand book after book of exegesis, and especially when it uses an *analogy* to *translate* the prayer shawl into its Greek equivalents, chlamys and chiton: "Throughout these days, a wholly visible sign expresses the underlying motif, namely, that for the individual, eternity is here shifted into time. For on these days the worshipper wears his shroud. It is true that even on ordinary days, the moment when the prayer shawl—chlamys and toga of antiquity—is donned, that moment directs the mind to the shroud, and to eternal life when God will sheath the soul in his mantle. Thus the weekday and the weekly Sabbath, as well as creation itself, illumine death as the crown and goal of creation. But the entire shroud, comprising not only the shawl but also the under-robe—chiton and tunic

of antiquity—is not the costume of every day. Death is the ultimate, the boundary of creation. Creation cannot encompass death as such. Only revelation has the knowledge—and it is the primary knowledge of revelation—that love is as strong as death. And so a man wears, already once in his life, on his wedding day under the bridal canopy, the complete shroud, which he has received from the hands of the bride" (*The Star of Redemption*, trans. William W. Hallo [London: Routledge, 1970], pp. 325–6).

I often wonder what is going through the mind of the enigmatic "Jewish fiancée" by Rembrandt (and Hélène Cixous's [*La fiancée juive—de la tentation*. Paris: Éditions des femmes, 1995]), with her two rings and her hand on the other's hand over her heart. Is she soon going to take the veil? A mourning veil, the veil of a bride or of a nun, or, for now, of a secular sister? What would she have thought if she'd read what comes next in Rosenzweig's text, at least up to the point where he talks about the "shroud," worn as "a challenge to death"; what would she have thought of this, for example, which comes shortly after the allusion to the "fiancée": "Only the man needs to be aware that the Torah is the basis of life. When a daughter is born, the father simply prays that he may lead her to the bridal canopy and to good works. For a woman has this basis of Jewish life for her own without having to learn it deliberately over and over, as the man who is less securely rooted in the depths of nature is compelled to do [well, that seems to recall—or rather to anticipate, for the lecture is later than Rosenzweig's text, though it is true that these statements are ageless—Freud's 'Femininity': woman closer to Nature, more rooted in it, for better and for worse]. According to ancient law, it is the woman who propagates Jewish blood. The child of a Jewish mother is Jewish by birth, just as the child of parents who are both Jewish" (Rosenzweig, p. 326).

13. See Catherine Chalier, *Judaïsme et altérité* (Paris: Verdier, 1982), p. 242: "Prayer, indeed, as 'promise of our lips' destined to 'replace the bulls,' must be as agreeable to God as the smell of the sacrifices. . . . ," specifies Catherine Chalier, whose words in quotation marks refer to Hosea, 14:2.

In Chouraqui's translation, the verses say: "Take with you the words and return to GOD./Say to him: 'Tolerate all the wrong and take what is good! /Let us pay the bullocks of our lips!'" [The Authorized version has: "Take with you words, and turn to the LORD: say unto him, Take away all iniquity, and receive *us* graciously: so will we render the calves of our lips," and the New Revised: "Take words with you and return to the LORD; say to him, 'Take away all guilt; accept that which is good, and we will offer the [bulls] of our lips.'"]

14. *Le vocabulaire des institutions indo-européennes* (Paris: Minuit, 1969), vol. 1, chap. 7, "Hospitality."

15. [Translator's note:] In English in the text.

16. *Kitsour Choul'hane Aroukh*, vol. 1, p. 45.

17. [Translator's note:] "*Et signe et livre et date*": taken verbally rather than nominally, this gives "sign(s) and deliver(s) and date(s)."

A Silkworm of One's Own, Chapter 3

1. Romans 2:25–9; see too Galatians 6:11–17 ("You see with what large letters I write with my hand! Those who wish to look good toward the flesh /oblige you to get yourselves circumcised,/with the sole aim of not being persecuted for the messiah's cross./No, those of circumcision do not themselves keep the torah;/but they want to have you circumcised so as to be proud of your flesh,/But for myself I am proud of nothing,/except the cross of our Adôn Ieshoua the messiah,/on which the universe was crucified for me and the universe. Yes circumcision is nothing, nor the foreskin, but a new creation" [trans. Chouraqui]). [Authorized version: "Ye see how large a letter I have written unto you with mine own hand./As many as desire to make a fair shew in the flesh, they constrain you to be circumcised; only lest they should suffer persecution for the cross of Christ./For neither they themselves who are circumcised keep the law; but desire to have you circumcised, that they may glory in your flesh./But God forbid that I should glory, save in the cross of our Lord Jesus Christ, by whom the world is crucified unto me, and I unto the world./For in Christ Jesus neither circumcision availeth any thing, nor uncircumcision, but a new creature"; New Revised: "See what large letters I make when I am writing in my own hand!/It is those who want to make a good showing in the flesh that try to compel you to be circumcised—only that they may not be persecuted for the cross of Christ./Even the

circumcised do not themselves obey the law, but they want you to be circumcised so that they may boast about your flesh./May I never boast of anything except the cross of our Lord Jesus Christ, by which the world has been crucified to me, and I to the world./For neither circumcision nor uncircumcision is anything; but a new creation is everything!"]

2. [Translator's note:] 1 Corinthians 11:3–10. Authorized version: "But I would have you know, that the head of every man is Christ; and the head of the woman is the man; and the head of Christ is God./Every man praying or prophesying, having his head covered, dishonoreth his head./But every woman that prayeth or prophesyeth with her head uncovered dishonoreth her head: for that is even all one as if she were shaven./For if the woman be not covered, let her also be shorn: but if it be a shame for a woman to be shorn or shaven, let her be covered./For a man indeed ought not to cover his head, forasmuch as he is the image and glory of God: but the woman of the man./Neither was the man created for the woman; but the woman for the man./For this cause ought the woman to have power on her head because of the angels." New Revised: "But I want you to understand that Christ is the head of every man, and the husband is the head of his wife, and God is the head of Christ. Any man who prays or prophesies with something on his head disgraces his head, but any woman who prays or prophesies with her head unveiled disgraces her head—it is one and the same thing as having her head shaved. For if a woman will not veil herself, then she should cut off her hair; but if it is disgraceful for a woman to have her hair cut off or to be shaved, she should wear a veil. For a man ought not to have his head veiled, since he is the image and reflection of God; but woman is the reflection of man. Neither was man created for the sake of woman, but woman for the sake of man. For this reason a woman ought to have a symbol of authority on her head, because of the angels."

3. Ibid., 13–15. [Authorized version: "Judge in yourselves: is it comely that a woman pray unto God uncovered?/Does not even nature itself teach you, that, if a man have long hair, it is a shame unto him?/But if a woman have long hair, it is a glory to her: for her hair is given her for a covering." New revised version: "Judge for yourselves: is it proper for a woman to pray to God with her head unveiled? Does not nature itself teach you that if a

man wears long hair, it is degrading to him, but if a woman has long hair, it is her glory? For her hair is given to her for a covering."]

4. [Translator's note:] This is an allusion to the ongoing *affaire des foulards* in the French school system, which has on several occasions controversially attempted to prevent Muslim girls from wearing the veil in school, in the name of the secular nature of the system as a whole.

5. 2 Corinthians 3:7. [Authorized version: "But if the ministration of death, written and engraven in stones, was glorious, so that the children of Israel could not steadfastly behold the face of Moses for the glory of his countenance; which glory was to be done away." New Revised version: "Now if the ministry of death, chiseled in letters on stone tablets, came in glory so that the people of Israel could not gaze at Moses' face because of the glory of his face, a glory now set aside . . ."]

6. Ibid., 3:12–18; 4:3–4. [Authorized version: "Seeing then that we have such hope, we use great plainness of speech:/And not as Moses, which put a vail over his face, that the children of Israel could not steadfastly look to the end of that which is abolished:/But their minds were blinded: for until this day remaineth the same vail untaken away in the reading of the old testament; which vail is done away in Christ./But even unto this day, when Moses is read, the vail is upon their heart./Nevertheless when it shall turn to the Lord, the vail shall be taken away. . . . But if our gospel be hid, it is hid to them that are lost:/in whom the god of this world hath blinded the minds of them which believe not." New Revised version: "Since, then, we have such a hope, we act with great boldness, not like Moses, who put a veil over his face to keep the people Israel from gazing at the end of the glory that was being set aside. But their minds were hardened. Indeed, to this very day, when they hear the reading of the old covenant, that same veil is still there, since only in Christ is it set aside. Indeed, to this day whenever Moses is read, a veil lies over their minds; but when one turns to the Lord, the veil is removed. . . . And even if our gospel is veiled, it is veiled to those who are perishing. In their case the god of this world has blinded the minds of the unbelievers."]

7. Walter Benjamin, *Das Passagen-Werk*, trans. Howard Eiland and Kevin McLaughlin as *The Arcades Project* (Cambridge, Mass. and London: Harvard University Press, 1999), N9, 6–8, p. 473.

8. [Editor's note:] "La double séance," in *La dissémination* (Paris: Seuil, 1972), especially around [Mallarmé's] *Crise de vers*, the "crisis . . . of the versus (V)" [*brise d'hiver, bise d'hiver, averse, vers, verre, envers, pervers, travers,* etc.], p. 310ff. and *passim.* It is recalled that this "versification" "deconstructs" the opposition of metaphor and metonymy (p. 314 n. 65).

Cultural Memory | in the Present

Richard Rand, ed., *Futures: Of Jacques Derrida*

William Rasch, *Niklas Luhmann's Modernity: The Paradoxes of Differentiation*

Jacques Derrida and Anne Dufourmantelle, *Of Hospitality*

Jean-François Lyotard, *The Confession of Augustine*

Kaja Silverman, *World Spectators*

Samuel Weber, *Institution and Interpretation: Expanded Edition*

Jeffrey S. Librett, *The Rhetoric of Cultural Dialogue: Jews and Germans in the Epoch of Emancipation*

Ulrich Baer, *Remnants of Song: Trauma and the Experience of Modernity in Charles Baudelaire and Paul Celan*

Samuel C. Wheeler III, *Deconstruction as Analytic Philosophy*

David S. Ferris, *Silent Urns: Romanticism, Hellenism, Modernity*

Rodolphe Gasché, *Of Minimal Things: Studies on the Notion of Relation*

Sarah Winter, *Freud and the Institution of Psychoanalytic Knowledge*

Samuel Weber, *The Legend of Freud: Expanded Edition*

Aris Fioretos, ed., *The Solid Letter: Readings of Friedrich Hölderlin*

J. Hillis Miller / Manuel Asensi, *Black Holes / J. Hillis Miller; or, Boustrophedonic Reading*

Miryam Sas, *Fault Lines: Cultural Memory and Japanese Surrealism*

Peter Schwenger, *Fantasm and Fiction: On Textual Envisioning*

Didier Maleuvre, *Museum Memories: History, Technology, Art*

Jacques Derrida, *Monolingualism of the Other; or, The Prosthesis of Origin*

Andrew Baruch Wachtel, *Making a Nation, Breaking a Nation: Literature and Cultural Politics in Yugoslavia*

Niklas Luhmann, *Love as Passion: The Codification of Intimacy*

Mieke Bal, ed., *The Practice of Cultural Analysis: Exposing Interdisciplinary Interpretation*

Jacques Derrida and Gianni Vattimo, eds., *Religion*